Angels:
What You Should Know about these Divine Messengers
(both the Good and the Bad)

.

by Jacob Quast

TODAY'S
REFORMATION
PRESS

Angels: What You Should Know about these Divine Messengers (both the Good and the Bad)
PUBLISHED BY TODAY'S REFORMATION PRESS
RR1 SITE2 BOX124
DE WINTON, ALBERTA
T0L 0X0

ISBN 978-0-9781785-3-6
Copyright © 2010 by Jacob Quast

All rights reserved - Today's Reformation Press., Inc.
No part of this publication may be reproduced or transmitted in any form or by any means, electronic or mechanical, including photocopying and recording, or by any information storage and retrieval system, without permission in writing from the publisher.

Quast, Jacob, 1977-
   Angels : what you should know about these divine
messengers (both the good and the bad) / by Jacob Quast.

Includes bibliographical references and index.
ISBN 978-0-9781785-3-6

   1. Angels. I. Title.
BL477.Q63 2010   202'.15   C2010-905012-6

Printed in the United States 2011
Cover image - © iStockphoto LP. All rights reserved.
Angel Appears to Balum, pg. 6 - © iStockphoto LP. All rights reserved.

www.todaysreformationpress.com

TABLE OF CONTENTS

Preface v
Introduction: 1
Chapter 1: Angels through the Christian Age 5
Chapter 2: Angels, Angels, Everywhere. 25
Chapter 3: Angelic Nature and Function 39
Chapter 4: Conclusion 53
Appendix A: Heirarchy of Angels 59
Appendix B: Rituals of Invocation. 61
Appendix C: Rituals of Evocation 65
Appendix D: Angel Stories 67
Bibliography 69
Index ....

FORWARD

When I was in Seminary, Jacob Quast would be seen nearly every day in his graduating year studying angels as he prepared his Master's thesis. It was at this time, I became aware of the value of Rev. Quasts work, as I learned that laymen and clergy need to be aware of the topic because of the growing interest and because of the dangers inherent in the growing New Age Movement. Accordingly, we are pleased at Today's Reformation Press Inc., to publish this book, *Angels: What You Should Know about these Divine Messengers (the Good and the Bad)* by Rev. Jacob Quast. Not only does this book provide insight into the increasing presence of Angelology in our local bookstore, he also provides a fantastic picture of what the Bible says about Angels, making this a valuable resource for all Christians and anyone who wants to explore the topic.

Sincerely,

Rev. Jay Holdner
Publisher - Today's Reformation Press, Inc.

PREFACE

The subject of angelology has always been a topic of fascination for people in the church; from the Early Church until now people have explored the nature and function of God's holy messengers. In recent years, however, there has also been a renewed interest concerning angels among people of all sorts of religious backgrounds in contemporary western culture. As the interest in the growing New Age Movement has developed so has the interest in angels. Many New Age writers advocate personal contact with these spiritual beings in order for people to improve their lives. Many different methods for making angelic contact are given, varying from writer to writer.

The Christian Church also has much to say regarding angels. Angels have always played a significant part in the area of Christian theology. They have served such important roles as God's messengers to His people, His children's protectors from harm and danger, as well as worshippers of the Heavenly Father. As people in the contemporary western culture seek fulfillment for their spiritual thirst in their pursuit of angels, the church has an opportunity to share the Biblical Word of the Gospel with these curious people.

Introduction

**I see that in every way you are very religious.
(Acts 17:22)[1]**

One may readily observe the decline of traditional faith in the twenty-first century western world, as well as the correlating increased interest in astrology, ouija boards, and other esoteric fortune-telling devices. Indeed, humans are rarely simple materialists. People yearn for something beyond this secular world, and if they do not find it in traditional religious faiths, they latch on to something else. Frequently, people have trouble believing in God. There may be many reasons for this, such as the troubling questions about God that have arisen following the incredible sufferings of the past one hundred years, disillusionment with the church, general secularism pervading the western worldview, as well as relativism (inherent in postmodernism) that avoids any claims of absolute truth.[2]

Today, in addition to the many other supernatural fascinations that many people have, there is a profound interest in angels. Bookstores abound with works on the subject of angels, and hundreds of titles relating to angels may be found within a single large bookstore. They also stock a wide variety of subjects relating to angels, from general information to artistic renderings of angels throughout history. Many books relate stories of angelic activity in people's lives or give instructions on how to make contact with one's personal angels. Though people may have difficulty believing in God, there is something appealing about contacting angels. Particularly with the great uncertainty and unrest that is pervasive throughout the world, there is something comforting about having the assurance that angels are guarding people.Yet, there are relatively few books which seek to explore the Biblical understanding of angels.[3]

Indeed, belief in angels has drastically changed over the last thirty years. In the first half of the twentieth century many people (even Christians) did not care to believe in angels at all. Due to the influence of modern theology, a sceptical attitude toward angels became prominent, though the degree to which a person was sceptical varied widely. Some allowed that the existence of good angels was possible, but maintained that there was no convincing proof of evil angels.[4] Now, however, there is widespread belief in angels among people, regardless of their religious orientation. In fact, the existence of good angels continues to be advocated by many, while the existence of evil angels is usually discounted as a product of the human mind.[5]

It is very difficult to decipher a coherent picture of New Age angelology because of the plethora of currently popular views.[6] Depictions of angels are prevalent in many different areas of western society. They are found on national newsmagazine covers, gift catalogues, and they are even stars on prime-time television.[7]

Prior to undertaking an analysis of angels in modern culture, as well as in the Bible, it is important to investigate the etymology of the term "angel." "Angel" is an English transliteration of the Greek word ἄγγελος, which in turn is roughly equivalent to the Hebrew word מַלְאָךְ. In Old Testament usage, the word מַלְאָךְ simply means "messenger." In Hebrew it could refer to a human messenger as one sent with a message, such as a prophet, priest, or other messenger from God who acted as an interpreter and declared what was right. Or it could also mean a spiritual or divine messenger from God, an angel.[8]

מַלְאָךְ (messenger) refers primarily to an individual who is sent by someone for the purpose of relaying a message or carrying out a specific duty. The messenger speaks, receives a response, and then returns to the one who sent him. It is very important to remember (especially in light of the popular views concerning angels) that in the Old Testament the messenger never reports his own message. His function and message are solely dependant upon the will of the person who sends him. He is significant not because of who he is, but because of who his superior is, the one who sent him.[9] "Therefore, a messenger of God is one whose message originates from and who is sent by God."[10]

To be sure, though human leaders frequently sent messengers for reasons of business or diplomacy (Genesis 32:3-6), God also sent prophetic or priestly messengers to His people (Haggai 1:13; Malachi 2:7). Though it is sometimes difficult to distinguish between human and angelic (spiritual) messengers of God (Judges 13:20; Malachi 3:1), nevertheless, angels serve as messengers of divine revelation in the Old Testament (Zechariah 1:13, 2:3).[11]

The word מַלְאָךְ is consistently translated as ἄγγελος in the Septuagint.[12] Primarily, the word ἄγγελος refers to spiritual beings sent by God. For ἄγγελος simply means one who brings a message (a messenger), as does מַלְאָךְ.[13] The New Testament writers continued with and emphasized the Old Testament Jewish view of angels as representatives of the heavenly world and messengers of God. Angels are seen to represent the other world. Indeed, the term ἄγγελος is used almost exclusively for divine, spiritual messengers, as the meaning of human messengers is given a relatively minor role.[14] Though ἄγγελος may refer to a human messenger (Mark 1:2), demonic powers as Satan's messengers or evil angels (Matthew 25:41), or heavenly ministers who oversee a group of believers under Jesus' supervision (Revelation 1:20, 2:1, 8, 12, 18) the term primarily refers, in the New Testament, to divine messengers and agents of God in terms of spiritual beings (Luke 1:26).[15]

Due to the increased general interest in angels, it is imperative to explore the current views concerning angelic origins and function, and to determine if and how they differ from the Scriptural perspective. This book will share the history of the Church's doctrine of angels, as well as provide a synthesis of the most prominent contemporary North American views, and an analysis of the Biblical standpoint.

I give thanks to you, my heavenly Father through Jesus Christ your dear Son, that you have protected me this night from all harm and danger, and I ask you that you would also protect me today from sin and all evil, so that my life and actions may please you completely. For into your hands I commend myself: my body, my soul, and all that is mine. Let your holy angel be with me, so that the wicked foe may have no power over me. Amen.[16]

Chapter Notes: Introduction

1. All Scripture references taken from the New International Version.
2. Michael Rogness, "A Fascination with Angels," *Word & World* 18, no. 1 (1998): 57-58.
3. Rogness, 58.
4. Francis Pieper, *Christian Dogmatics*, vol. 1 (St. Louis: Concordia Publishing House, 1950), 497.
5. Paul Roland, *Angels: A Piatkus Guide* (London: Judy Piatkus Publishers, Ltd., 1999), 63.
6. Duane A. Garrett, *Angels and the New Spirituality* (Nashville: Broadman & Holman Publishers, 1995), 132-133.
7. Stephen F. Noll, *Angels of Light, Powers of Darkness: Thinking Biblically About Angels, Satan, & Principalities* (Downers Grove, IL: InterVarsity Press, 1998), 11-12.
8. Francis Brown, "מַלְאָךְ," in The *New Brown—Driver—Briggs—Gesenius Hebrew and English Lexicon with an Appendix Containing the Biblical Aramaic* (N.P.: Christian Copyrights, Inc., 1983), 521.
9. D.N. Freedman and B.E. Willoughby, "מַלְאָךְ," in Theo*logical Dictionary of the Old Testament*, ed. G.J. Botterweck, Helmer Ringgren, and Heinz-Josep Fabry, trans. Douglas W. Stott, vol. 8 (Grand Rapids: Wm. B. Eerdmans Publishing Co., 1997), 309.
10. Freedman and Willoughby, 315.
11. Stephen F. Noll, "מַלְאָךְ," in New *International Dictionary of Old Testament Theology and Exegesis*, ed. Willem A. VanGemeren, vol. 2 (Grand Rapids: Zondervan Publishing House, 1997), 941-942.
12. Freedman and Willoughby, 309.
13. Walter Grundmann, "ἄγγελος in the Greek and Hellenistic World," in *Theological Dictionary of the New Testament*, ed. Gerhard Kittel and Geoffrey W. Bromiley, trans. Geoffrey W. Bromiley, vol. 1 (Grand Rapids: Wm. B. Eerdmans Publishing Co., 1964), 74.
14. Gerhard Kittel, "ἄγγελος in the NT," in *Theological Dictionary of the New Testament*, ed. Gerhard Kittel and Geoffrey W. Bromiley, trans.Geoffrey W. Bromiley, vol. 1 (Grand Rapids: Wm. B. Eerdmans Publishing Co., 1964), 83.
15. "ἄγγελος" in *Analytical Lexicon of the Greek New Testament*, ed. Timothy Friberg, Barbara Friberg, and Neva F. Miller (Grand Rapids: Baker Books, 2000), 31.
16. Small Catechism VI.2, in *The Book of Concord*, ed. Robert Kolb and Timothy J. Wengert (Minneapolis: Fortress Press, 2000), 363.

1

Angels Through the Christian Age

"For by Him all things were created: things in heaven and on earth, visible and invisible, whether thrones or powers or rulers or authorties; all things were created by Him and for Him." (Colossians 1:16)

The church has been fascinated for millennia with angels as they are closely connected to both God and mankind by being their servants.[1] This chapter shall briefly summarize the major beliefs and controversies concerning angels since the time of the Early Church. Due to the enormous variety of beliefs the discussion will not be exhaustive. However, suggestions for further reading in this area will be provided at appropriate places within the chapter.

6 ▪ Chapter 1

The angel appears to Balaam
Engraving by Gustave Dore (1832 – 1883)

Commonly published in "bible or books of New testament
and Old testament"(1875)
scan by Ivan Burmistrov

THE EARLY CHURCH (A.D. 100–600)

There are descriptions of angels in the Bible from the beginning of Genesis[2] to the end of Revelation.[3] Accordingly the dogma concerning angels quickly began to develop within the church, especially to combat false views concerning the nature and function of angels. With Romans 1:25 in mind, Robert Jenson writes, "Throughout Scripture it is humanity's great fall that we have worshiped...the creature rather than the Creator."[4] There are even hints in the New Testament that some were "assigning to angels an importance independent of their function as messengers and servants of God."[5] This unwholesome attitude toward angels continued into the early church, and it fell to the church's theologians to formulate Scriptural responses to unscriptural teachings and attitudes common among the people of their time.

It is evident that the development of the dogma concerning angels was a slow and evolving process. Origen asserts that the early church did not have an established doctrine of angels, but did make some declarations regarding them.[6] The world of the early church was so spirit-conscious that it was not necessary for theologians to prove the existence of angels, but they did need to clarify their true nature and functions. This was usually accomplished by citing a passage from Scripture to prove their point, but even this was not a high priority.[7]

Early theologians such as Justin Martyr, Athenagoras, Origen, and Jerome considered angels a subject worthy of Christian thought and confession. They affirmed the Biblical teachings that angels are God's servants and that guardian angels exist; and they viewed the decisive function of angels as worship. In fact, it was only through fusion into the greater order of the heavenly liturgy that the earthly liturgy was able to be heard. The closest earthly liturgy to that of the angels was the daily hymns of the monks, consisting of the constant repetition of the offices and forbearance of any musical instruments apart from the human voice.[8]

The angelic nature was thought to be primarily spiritual and their function to be as servants. Some theologians, such as Lactantius, went further in formulating angelic dogma by stating that angels are finite spiritual creatures whose primary purpose is to serve. They are incorporeal, invisible, intangible, insoluble, indestructible, intelligent created beings (with limited knowledge), and, depending upon their mission from God, they may appear in physical form (generally as young winged men), though this occurrence is rare. Angels usually minister to God, but they are also His instruments in carrying out His will on earth.[9] However, many theologians sought to discover the existence and nature of angels elsewhere than in the Holy Scriptures.[10] This practise of philosophical speculation led to divisions within the church concerning the doctrine of angels.

Divisions also arose within the church due to the misguided beliefs associated with common folk piety,[11] as well as the Gnostic influence that permeated early Christianity.[12] At times, in their zeal to defend their Christian faith, some theologians inadvertently caused confusion regarding angels. For example, Justin Martyr, while refuting a charge of atheism brought against the church by the Romans, places angels very close to God. Athenagoras also made a similar statement, while discussing the doctrine of God, which gave the impression that there was a similarity between the nature of God and that of angels. Though the official teaching of the church stated that angels were created servants of God, questions regarding the time of their creation and the very nature of their existence were left open to investigation and speculation.[13]

Due to this openness regarding angelology, strange and anti-Scriptural views were often espoused. Prior to the Council of Nicea it was common to describe Christ, and even the Holy Spirit, as an "angel." This, combined with the popular notion that angels helped to create the world, contributed to advance Arius' teaching (based upon such passages as Proverbs 8:22-31 and Hebrews 1:4) that Jesus was an actual angel and not true God. In Arian terminology it was acceptable to call angels "sons of God" (according to Genesis 6:1) or to refer to the Son of God as an angel. This angelic Christology found in Arianism had its roots in late Jewish and early Christian apocalypticism and seems to have originated as an attempt to take a stand against what was perceived to be a new, hellenized Christology.[14]

Another practice that became popular in the early church was the worshiping of angels. In the fourth and fifth centuries, the common people began to venerate martyrs as saints. Pieces of the cross and bones of the saints became prized as holy relics which could aid people in their spiritual journey. People sought the intercessions of the saints on their behalf—especially those of Mary, the mother of Jesus—though some church leaders (including Eusebius of Caesarea, and Epiphanius) tried to stop this movement. At the same time that saints began to be venerated, so too did angels. They were even worshiped with religious honours as the guardians of towns, cities, and nations against danger and calamity. Some theologians (such as Jerome and Augustine) clearly distinguished between the qualified homage due celestial beings (saints and angels) and the proper worship of God.[15]

However, differences of opinion among theologians led to confusion among the common people. For example, while Jerome and Augustine differentiated between the homage due to angels and to God, Gregory I affirmed the belief that "a main ground of hope is the intercession of perfected saints and angels."[16] Though the early church officially condemned the practise of angel-veneration, the common people were nevertheless confirmed in their belief that angels heard and answered prayer by the church's practise of dedicating churches to angels. The common people were given conflicting statements by various church theologians regarding the appropriateness of invoking angelic aid, irregardless of any theological explanations designed to clarify the issue.[17]

There arose in the early church a controversy about whether or not good angels are permanently in a state of goodness. Some theologians held that angels are not confirmed in a state of goodness until after the Last Judgement.[18] Gregory of Nazianzum (also referred to as Gregory of Nazianzus) and Cyril of Jerusalem believed that the good angels who at first resisted temptation may yet succumb and fall. Yet, as another illustration of how divided clergy were concerning angelic doctrine, Augustine and Gregory the Great vigorously disagreed with Cyril and Gregory.[19]

In conjunction with this idea of angels falling into sin and temptation, another interesting idea was advanced by Justin Martyr, Tatian, Athenagoras, and Lactantius, who ascribed to angels a body of fine ethereal matter, but matter nevertheless. They believed that because angels could be punished and fall into sin it was necessary that they have a material body of some kind. This was due in large part to the influence of Greek philosophy, which did not believe that pure spirit could sin. Therefore, logically speaking, if angels could and had sinned and could be punished, they must have a physical body of some sort. An outgrowth of this Greek idea that the pure spirit could not sin was the idea that the human soul was trapped in the physical body. However, the church's theologians did clearly state that the soul was not an angel entrapped by flesh. Indeed the human soul and angels are two separate things, not to be confused.[20]

Another concept regarding fallen angels which became hotly debated in the early church was the idea first proposed by Origen that perhaps the devil and fallen angels would eventually be restored. This notion was later advanced by Didymus of Alexandria and Gregory of Nyssa, but was vigorously opposed by Jerome and Augustine. However, it was not until the sixth century that this error was officially condemned by Emperor Justinian.[21]

It was also during this period in the church's history that the idea of a heavenly, angelic hierarchy was promulgated. The fifth century theologian Pseudo-Dionysius (also known as Dionysius the Areopagite, who was taken to be the Apostle Paul's disciple, and therefore whose works were given almost Scriptural authority)[22] taught that communion with God occurs through a process of illumination and purification, which is carried out by means of the heavenly hierarchy. This heavenly hierarchy consisted, after

God, of nine orders or choirs of angels, further divided into three general ranks,[23] to which correspond the three orders of hierarchy on earth (See Appendix A for differing arrangements of the angelic orders posed by various Latin writers). It was by this complex system of symbols that a soul climbed up to a direct union with God.[24] Therefore, the precise purpose of angels in this system was that of assisting mankind to attain the kingdom of heaven.

The final controversy to be discussed here addresses the time of the creation of angels. Scripture does not explicitly state when angels were created. Thus this question fell into the realm of allowable speculation and investigation. Gregory of Nazianzum believed angels were created prior to the rest of the world. He was opposed by Augustine and others who dated the angels' creation to the first day. The question grew in importance in the church as the idea became popular that angels had actually assisted in creating the world. Though the early fathers clearly condemned this teaching, it continued to be debated and discussed until the church was finally forced to compose a creedal statement regarding this matter.[25]

It was with many of these controversies in mind that the theologians gathered at Nicea in A.D. 325 to discuss the most pertinent and potentially damaging ideas in the realm of angelology including the eternal existence of angels and the Arian view that Jesus was an actual angel, both of which were fairly common prior to this Council.[26] Jaroslav Pelikan notes:

That official tradition was canonized as dogma when the Council of Nicea adopted a confession that went beyond the simple thetical statements of creation in other creeds to specify that God was maker not only of heaven and earth, but of 'all things visible and invisible.' Speculation about angelology was not cut off, but in its doctrine of creation the church set a limit beyond which such speculation could not be permitted to go.[27]

This open invitation into the realm of speculation led to the necessity of continued dogmatic statements by the church regarding the origin and function of angels. For example, the Council of Laodicea, c. A.D. 360, forbade the worship of angels. It sought to draw a line between homage, which was acceptable, and the rendering of divine honours, which was forbidden (it being appropriate to give such honours only to God, not created beings).[28]

Certainly more could be said about angels in the early church. However, these controversies were the most widely discussed and provide a solid basis for future discussion regarding the view of angels in the following time periods. Obviously there were various ideas being circulated regarding angels, as there are today. As these opposing ideas took root and developed in Christian thought, it became necessary at times for the church to respond to anti-Scriptural ideas which threatened to undermine the Biblical record concerning angels. This trend has continued in the church throughout the ages.[29]

THE MIDDLE AGE (A.D. 600–1300)

"The theology of the medieval schools, known as scholasticism, was remarkable for the thoroughness with which the details of Christian doctrine were worked out and systematized."[30] Indeed, during the period of the Middle Ages, angelology became a central topic in theology. The scholastics frequently speculated regarding the nature of angels. Nevertheless, most of the questions concerning angels (such as their means of locomotion) were not articles of faith. There were just two significant questions of faith in relation to angels: their creation, and the confirmation of good angels.[31]

In regard to the question of their creation, some theologians such as Bonaventure held to the Greek fathers' notion that angels existed prior to the creation of the physical world. However, other theologians such as Thomas Aquinas held that angels were not created prior to the physical world.[32] Aquinas also held that angels had been created with corporeal creatures and that they were innumerable. Aquinas believed that their function consisted primarily of attaining eternal happiness and glorifying God; secondarily, they might help and protect men and rule over corporeal creatures.[33]

In regard to the second question of faith, concerning the confirmation of the good angels, though there was no explicit Biblical affirmation, the idea was widely supported that after the fall of the angels and of Adam and Eve, God confirmed those angels who had remained true to Him. He accomplished this through His grace and glory so that they are no longer able to fall, a benefit that provided them, as well as their human charges, with protection. This was deemed to be cooperating grace, whereby the angels were no longer able to sin, although their free choice remained.[34]

Based upon Scripture, the church was able to formulate a statement of faith only relating to angelic creation. Pope Innocent III, at the Fourth Lateran Council of A.D. 1215, pronounced the doctrine that angels are simply spiritual beings, created holy. This continued the trend, begun in the early church, of leaving angelology completely open to speculation. Consequently, a wide range of views remained, expanding upon the nature and office of angels.[35] Even though scholasticism theorized widely and freely about angels, the church councils and church doctrine continued to be reticent on the subject. For example, the Council of Lyons in A.D. 1274 contented itself with a "re-affirmation of the opening statement of the Nicene Creed."[36]

In the Middle Ages, due to the wide freedom that the scholastics were granted in regard to angelic speculation, much philosophical debate took place that was later considered to be ridiculous, such as the infamous question as to how many angels can dance on the head of a pin.[37] However, much of the dialogue in the Middle Ages was a continuation and further development of issues that arose in the early church, such as the angelic hierarchy. Angelology and ecclesiology were closely connected because both were founded upon a hierarchical definition of reality. Indeed, there was a parallel between the celestial and ecclesiastical hierarchies formulated by the mystical theologian Pseudo-Dionysius.[38]

The writings of Pseudo-Dionysius, especially the *Celestial Hierarchy*, expanded the treatment of angels both theologically and spiritually. It set the dominant pattern for the treatment of angels throughout the Middle Ages. Ewert H. Cousins states:

> The *Celestial Hierarchy* ushered into Christian spirituality a notion that had a transforming effect, namely that of angelic hierarchy. The term means a holy principle, but in reference to the angels it meant an organizational pattern in which groups of angels were arranged in a descending or ascending order in accordance to one's perspective, for example, seraphim (love), cherubim, (knowledge), thrones (forever in the divine presence), dominions (benevolent rule), powers (courage), authorities (lift up inferior angels), principalities (manifest transcendent principles), archangels (interpreters of divine enlightenment), and angels (revelation to the world). These nine levels provide the framework of the human spiritual journey. Angelic spirituality, then, consists largely in the awakening of these levels in the human person and in the movement of the soul to greater union with God. This is accomplished through the direct ministry of angels and through the correspondences latent in the soul that can be awakened in the spiritual journey.[39]

Bernard of Clairvaux espoused the common belief that along the spiritual journey of the soul to enter into union and love with God, there are many detours and dead ends. Yet, along these spiritual pathways there are many helpers to give people guidance and protection. Angels are among these helpers. "Angels guide men and women along the many pathways of Christian faith in ways that not only circumvent the dead-end voids but serve to reveal God as *all in all* (cf. 1 Corinthians 15:28)."[40] Also, angels serve as examples for mankind to follow. They assist us in our endeavour to remain on the proper path through humility and self-knowledge by imitating their ways as they follow their own pathways of ascent and descent to God.[41]

Once again, much more could be said regarding the dogma of angels in the Middle Ages, especially due to the wide range of speculation that occurred among the scholastics. However, the preceding discussion has served to illustrate the most pertinent points regarding the nature and function of angels.[42]

THE REFORMATION (A.D. 1300–1700)

During the Reformation, both Protestants and Roman Catholics continued to believe in the real existence of angels and demons, basing this belief upon the Holy Scriptures.[43] In fact, the Reformation dogma of angels tended to repeat medieval thought (just as the Middle Ages tended to repeat the thought of the early church), but with somewhat less detail. Actually, the Reformers did not come under attack by the Roman Catholic Church concerning their dogma of angels until the seventeenth century, and then largely "because of [their (the Reformers)] interpretation of the doctrine of the fall of the evil angels in light of Calvinist views of predestination and reprobation."[44] Due to the plethora of views regarding angels held by the equally numerous "reformers" of the church during this period, only the beliefs of Martin Luther, Martin Chemnitz, and John Calvin will be discussed.

The Reformers believed steadfastly in the importance of belief in angels. Lutherans celebrated a church festival of angels so that the people could know and learn about good and bad angels. This was important because evil angels were an ever-present reality and the church leaders found it pertinent, for the well-being of their flocks, to remember that, though Satan is trying to devour people like a lion (1 Peter 5:8), God has given His people good angels to protect and preserve them (Psalm 34:7).[45]

Martin Luther did not have much to say regarding the nature of angels, other than that they are the most exalted of created beings. He affirmed that they are spiritual beings, created in connection with the world and not before. At first, like man, they were not so well-established in their faith that they could not have sinned—hence the Devil's failure to abide in the truth. However, those who did remain true could—after a certain point—no longer sin. Luther also pointed out that angels have great power of their own, which is derived from their perpetual fellowship with God. Due to their close relationship with God (they stand in His very presence) they are much more powerful than the devils. Luther did not concern himself with idle conjectures regarding the supposed angel hierarchy first formulated by Pseudo-Dionysius, beyond holding that Cherubim and Seraphim are really just different descriptions of how angels may appear, not terms denoting different kinds of angels. He did not view it as a matter of human concern to investigate the inner-relations that took place in the angel world.[46]

It was Martin Chemnitz, in his *Loci Theologici*, who clearly defined the origin and nature of angels. He held it to be manifest from the Bible that angels were indeed created beings (Colossians 1:16). However, because there is no description in Genesis of their creation, there had been much debate concerning when they were created. Some believed that they were created out of nothing, before heaven and earth were formed. Others held that the account of their creation fell under the word "heaven." Still others believed that they were created on the second day of creation, when some immediately fell because God did not see that the second day was good. Chemnitz believed, on the basis of Job 38:4-7, that angels were created before humans, but since the exact time and place has not been revealed in Scripture people do not, and cannot, ever know more for certain.[47]

Nonetheless, Chemnitz clearly laid out what can be known concerning angelic origins. Angels did not exist by themselves and were not begotten of the substance of God, but were created (before humans, though not from eternity). According to Daniel 10:3, they are not omnipresent (as is God). They are invisible creatures (Colossians 1:16 and 20), spirits (Hebrews 1:14) who do not have flesh and bones (Luke 24:39 and Ephesians 6:12). All angels were created in truth (John 8:44), in holiness, in righteousness, and in the image of God, which is yet to be restored in mankind (Ephesians 4:24).[48]

However, some angels fell out of God's truth, invariably and irrevocably changing their nature. They are now lying and murdering sinners. They who once were free are now bound in chains forever. No longer are they in the light, but in darkness. Jude writes that some angels did not keep their original authority (verse 6). According to 2 Peter 2:4 there are many devils (fallen angels) who are without hope of restoration.[49]

Yet Chemnitz affirms, as did Luther, that those angels who remained in God's truth have been so strengthened that they are now elect and can no longer fall (1 Timothy 5:21). The nature of these good angels has many facets. They are steadfast in truth; they see the face of God (Matthew 18:10), thereby enjoying eternal bliss; they know God and His will (Ephesians 3:10); they adore and praise God (Isaiah 6:3 and Hebrews 1:6); they attend and serve God (Daniel 7:10); and they are sent to minister to the faithful (Hebrews 1:14). Again, they cannot fall into sin or death, as will also be the case for Christians after Christ's return, when they will be "like angels" (Luke 20:36). Also, as with Luther, Chemnitz deigns not to investigate deeply the supposed "celestial hierarchy." He holds that only the Creator knows the precise difference among the angels.[50]

Concerning the function of angels, Martin Luther held that angels were created to serve and minister to mankind, and people were to thank God for them. For God protects and aids believers through His angels—otherwise all manner of bad things would continually happen to them because the devil is constantly trying to inflict hurt upon them.[51] Nonetheless, God does at times permit His people to experience bad things so that they might know what things would be like if He was not protecting them continuously, and so be moved to give thanks for His gracious provision of protection through His holy angels. God does allow the devil free reign and power over His people at times in order to chastise them, with the intention of drawing them back to Himself.[52]

Luther believed it important for all people to remember that "should our Lord recall the angels, not one of us would survive, but all would be dead in a moment."[53] Yet, mankind is given hope because the devil is unable to do any more harm than what God permits or allows him (as in the example of Job). Evil angels are eager to cause harm to people's bodies, possessions, and souls through malevolence, hatred, anger, arrogance, et cetera, in order to bring them down to hell. However, it is the divine purpose and function of good angels to guard and protect people like a wall against the devil and his minions. Angels oppose the evil spirits and devils. They are kind, merciful, benevolent spirits who prevent the demons from doing all that they would like to do. In fact, God has ordained that each Christian has not just one, but many angels to look after and protect him.[54]

In regard to guardian angels, Luther's later theology postulated that only Christians had appointed angels to watch over them. The person who does not fear God when trouble comes his way will not be protected by angels.[55] Nevertheless, Luther also adopted the idea that everyone has a guardian angel. He says that "if the beloved angels were not always there standing guard over and protecting us, we could well succumb to death ten times over in just one hour."[56] He had earlier held that not only to every Christian, but to every human being, government, city, and country there is a special angel assigned.[57] Luther also writes: "Thus it is with all men when they escape misfortune or have good fortune: it is all the work of God and the angels."[58]

To combat the devil, angels are always actively working all around people. They awaken thoughts within mankind and may also confront people externally with reasons and warnings. Angels do not preserve creation from within, but work externally upon creation in a more protective fashion.[59] Chemnitz describes the great battle that is taking place between good and evil angels—on our account. Those evil angels that have been cast out of heaven now encircle us on earth, constantly trying to undermine the church, the state, and Christian households. The devil moves the ungodly to try and bring harm to believers because they are captive to his will. His evil angels lie in wait for individuals in order to bring harm to them, in both body and soul, using both temporal and spiritual weapons. Yet, though he is allowed to lay siege to people physically, though he seeks them and demands a right to them as a trophy of war because of their sin, God yet fights for them. Christ the Lord takes the field to do battle, commanding His angelic hosts. Angels literally surround believers in order to protect them—and they are stronger than the devil and his minions, because Christ is the strong one who has bound Satan.[60]

Chemnitz lists many other functions of the holy angels. In the church, angels aid the ministry of the Word; the Law was given through angels (Galatians 3:19); the Gospel was announced to Mary by Gabriel (Luke 1:30). Through the church, the wisdom of God is made known to the angels (Ephesians 3:10). Also, angels are present at church meetings (1 Corinthians 11:10). However, good angels are also present with the secular rulers (Daniel 6 and 10 and Isaiah 37:36).

Angels also help protect people in their households (Tobit 8:3). Angels protect as well as bestow physical blessings, as is shown by the rescue of Lot in Genesis by two angels. Angels also help Christians spiritually by carrying their prayers to God (Tobit 12:12), by praying on Christians' behalf (Zechariah 1:12 and Acts 10:3-4), and by joining their prayers with believers' (Revelation 8:3-4).[61]

John Calvin, in his angelology, held that angels do exist. They are spiritual servants of God and were created as creatures higher than man. However, angels are not to be worshiped. He also held to the Scriptural belief that demons are fallen angels. Demons were not evil by nature but by virtue of their sinful corruption. He emphatically stated that demons are personal beings and not man's own evil inclinations. Along with Luther and Chemnitz, Calvin did not follow Pseudo-Dionysius into the realm of speculation concerning angelic hierarchies.[62]

Angels were not a high theological priority for Calvin because he held that "the only way in which angels communicate with us is through the intercession of Christ, and therefore one ought to be more concerned about the knowledge of Christ than about knowledge of angels."[63] It is interesting, though, that the majority of Calvin's discussion is centered upon demons, not angels, both because the knowledge of demons and how they act was important for the Christian life and because the question of Satan and fallen angels, and their relationship to the will of God, is intrinsically connected with issues of the divine will and predestination.[64]

It is readily apparent how widespread was the belief in the existence in angels and demons in the Reformation period. It is also readily apparent that the divergence in views regarding the dogma of angelic nature and function continued into this period as well. While the basic belief in angels, as found in Scripture, was adhered to by most people, the particulars of this doctrine were still open to speculation (as they had been in the early church and Middle Ages), though there was more of an effort on the part of the Reformers to establish their dogma on the basis of Scripture (as Martin Chemnitz often did). However, though there was indeed at this time a fascination with the spirit world, especially in regard to the fallen angels, it is interesting to note that the symbolical books developed in this era make only passing references to these dogmas.[65] However, this fascination with the spirit world (in regard to Biblical teaching) was soon to come to an end in the next period of human history.[66]

THE ENLIGHTENMENT (A.D. 1700–1800)

There is really very little to say about angelology during the Enlightenment. It was during this time that belief in angels almost completely disappeared, due primarily to the impact of rationalism on theology (at least, among scholarly circles). Those who did believe in angels on account of Scripture did not really know what to believe about them.[67] Though belief was present, it had little depth.

The church's indifference regarding this dogma left the area open for speculation in unprecedented directions by certain individuals. Such was the case with Emmanuel Swedenborg, founder of what is known today as the Swedenborgian cult, who, in the eighteenth century, speculated much about the angelic world. He believed that angels were not a separate classification of created spiritual beings, but were glorified men. Nor did he believe in the existence of Satan. The information that he gathered on angels was allegedly received by his own personal interactions and conversations with angels.[68]

Even in this period of scepticism regarding angels, there was still in existence a disturbing trend in the area of angel magic that had begun many years earlier. The 'Treatises of Dr. Rudd' comprise Mss Harley 6481-6486 in the British Library and are copies made by a certain Peter Smart in the period 1699-1714. They are compilations of esoteric material from the early seventeenth century and show that exploration of the Hermetic (esoteric teaching of occult sciences, including magic and alchemy) tradition continued into the early eighteenth century.[69]

What is most interestingly revealed in this manuscript is the unabated belief in the power and sovereignty of God by those who performed angel magic. Dr. Rudd explains in great detail how to identify the conjured spirit as a "good" angel. This is important because one would not want to come into contact with an "evil" spirit. Magicians often invoked spirits without any great inner qualms. This is because they saw these spirits as part of God's creation and so worthy of their attention.[70] "The earliest *grimoires*, the books of conjuration, describe elevated spiritual rituals that would not be out of place in any religious tradition, requiring fasting, abstention and a period of celibacy, prayers to God, purification and remission of sins, and petitions and addresses to the supreme God, in whose name they undertook their occult work."[71]

The magicians sought to contact only "Celestial Angels and other dignified Elemental powers and spirits of light by nature and office wholly benevolent and good, [who] may not be commanded nor constrained by any invocation. They are only to be moved and called forth by humble entreaties thereby acquiring favour and friendship."[72] The magician was also obligated to vanquish any evil spirits or powers of darkness, firstly by the name of the most High God, and finally, failing that, by calling upon the name of Jesus.[73] However, they were also able to command "all sublunary spirits and powers of all natures, orders and offices, both good and evil, light and darkness, or otherwise relating thereunto and bring them to such obedience, as according to their several and respective natures and office they may be so commanded and constrained to serve and obey."[7]

THE MODERN ERA (A.D 1800-CA.1970)

The modern era continued the trend begun in the Enlightenment of sceptical indifference among many Christians in regard to angels. Friedrich Scleiermacher taught that it was acceptable to believe in angels privately, but since they are so far outside man's realm of experience there is no reason to inquire into the specifics of their creation, nature, or activities. None of this is pertinent to salvation. He believed that angelology was outside of, and even problematic to, the study of Dogmatics.[75] Schleiermacher stated that "the only tenet which can be established as a doctrine concerning angels is this: that the question whether the angels exist or not ought to have no influence upon our conduct, and that revelations of their existence are now no longer to be expected."[76]

Schleiermacher's primary defect in regard to angelology (as well as that of many other theologians at the time) was the heavy influence that rationalism had on how he viewed the Bible. The Bible, which until the age of the Enlightenment had been held in the highest regard, now lacked credibility to a great many people. They could not believe in angels or demons because they could not accept the Biblical accounts as convincing proof. For example, the dogma concerning the devil was summarily rejected because it simply went against reason that perfectly good angels would choose to fall away and reject their Creator.[77] "That this conception is losing its influence among Christians follows naturally from the fact that it belongs to a time when our knowledge of the forces of nature was very limited, and our power over them at its lowest stage. In every such situation our reflections now instinctively take another direction, so that in active life we do not easily turn to angels."[78]

Yet many Christians did continue in their belief in angels as revealed in Scripture. In the late nineteenth century, Alexander Whyte said in a sermon to his congregation that angels are "ministering spirits sent forth from the Son's throne to minister to those He has redeemed, to those who are to be heirs of salvation."[79] However, the depth of investigation into this area of theology was often very shallow.

The belief in the non-existence of angels was prevalent right into the twentieth century. Edward Koehler writes in his *Summary of Christian Doctrine*, "also, in our day there are those who doubt and even deny the existence of angels, especially of the devil. Indeed, we find no evidence of their existence in nature, but numerous texts of the Bible definitely prove that angels do exist."[80] Koehler affirms from the Bible that angels are created, spiritual beings. The function of the good angels consists of giving willing and joyful service unto God. They praise and worship Him as well as carry out His commandments. They are especially called upon to promote the work of Christ's church and to protect her servants.[81]

Koehler also refuted the misconception common among modern theologians that evil angels are merely a personification of the evil in man or in the world. He held that they too are personal spiritual beings. Their sole purpose is to attempt to destroy the works of God and to counteract His gracious intervention towards mankind. They seek to hurt and harm believers, with the intention of leading them or others away from the truth, which is in Jesus. However, they are under God's sovereign power and can do no more harm than He allows.[82]

The persistent apathy towards the doctrine of angels continued largely unabated for many years. While doing research for her book on angels in the late 1970s, Hope MacDonald found a total of eight books on angels in bookstores throughout the Chicago area. However, in keeping with the trend begun in the early church with a fascination towards evil angels, she found many hundreds of books on demons and the occult.[83] The following chapter will discuss the complete reversal of this trend. There are literally thousands of current books which have angelology as the primary subject matter. The large range of ideas that are divergent from Scripture will be discussed and analyzed. Though there are many books being written about angels, what is being written is key. Unfortunately, many of these ideas are in direct contradiction to the Biblical revelation concerning God's spiritual messengers.

> *God himself is present; hear the harps resounding; see the hosts the throne surrounding!'Holy, holy, holy!' Hear the hymn ascending, songs of saints and angels blending.*[84]

Chapter Notes: Chapter 1

1. Karl Barth, Church Dogmatics, vol. 3, *The Doctrine of Creation*, ed. G.W. Bromiley and T.F. Torrance, trans. G.W. Bromiley and R.J. Ehrlich, part 3 (Edinburgh: T & T Clark Ltd., 1983), 371.
2. Genesis 3:24, which describes the cherubim guarding the entrance to Eden after the Fall, is the first *explicit* mention of angels in the Bible.
3. Revelation 22:8 is the Apostle John's final conversation with the angel who has guided him on his heavenly journey (and to whom he inadvertently bows down to worship).
4. Robert W. Jenson, *Systematic Theology*, vol. 2, *The Works of God* (New York: Oxford University Press, 1999), 112.
5. Jaroslav Pelikan, *The Christian Tradition: A History of the Development of Doctrine*, vol. 1, *The Emergence of the Catholic Tradition* (100-600) (Chicago: University of Chicago Press, 1971), 133.
6. K.R. Hagenbach, *History of Doctrines*, vol. 1, trans. Henry B. Smith (New York: Sheldon and Company, 1861), 139.
7. Emil Schneweis, *Angels and Demons According to Lactantius* (Washington, D.C.: The Catholic University of America Press, Inc., 1944), 17, 19.
8. Barth, 381, 383-384.
9. Schneweis, 30-32, 37, 46, 49, 51, 60.
10. Barth, 384.
11. There existed among the common people an idea that angels were a kind of "lesser god." See Alexander Roberts, trans., "Irenaeus Against Heresies," 2.2.1, in *The Ante-Nicene Fathers: Translations of the Writings of the Fathers down to A.D. 325*, vol. 1, *The Apostolic Fathers—Justin Martyr—Irenaeus*, edited by Alexander Roberts and James Donaldson (Grand Rapids: Wm. B. Eerdmans Publishing Company, 1981), 361.
12. One popular Gnostic teaching was that angels were creators of the world. See F. Crombie, trans., "The Pastor of Hermas: Visions," 3.4.1, in *The Ante-Nicene Fathers: Translations of the Writings of the Fathers down to A.D. 325*, vol. 2, *Fathers of the Sceond Century: Hermas, Tatian, Athenagoras, Theophilus, and Clement of Alexandria (Entire)*, edited by Alexander Roberts and James Donaldson (Grand Rapids: Wm. B. Eerdmans Publishing Company, 1979), 14.

13. Pelikan, 1:134.
14. Pelikan, 1:140, 190-191.
15. George Park Fisher, *History of Christian Doctrine* (New York: Charles Scribner's Sons, 1896), 172.
16. Fisher, 198.
17. Hagenbach, 1:338.
18. Schneweis, 55.
19. Hagenbach, 1:341.
20. Schneweis, 38-39, 41.
21. Hagenbach, 1:342.
22. Justo L. Gonzalez, *A History of Christian Thought*, vol. 2, rev. ed., *From Augustine to the Eve of the Reformation* (Nashville: Abingdon Press, 1971), 93.
23. This angelic hierarchy consisted of Seraphim, Cherubim, and Thrones in the first category; Dominions, Powers, and Authorities in the second; and Principalities, Archangels, and Angels in the third.
24. Fisher, 173.
25. Hagenbach, 1:139, 338.
26. Schneweis, 21.
27. Pelikan, 1:135.
28. Fisher, 124.
29. For more information regarding the early church's views on angels see Jaroslav Pelikan's *The Christian Tradition: A History of the Development of Doctrine*, vol. 1 and *Angels and Demons According to Lactantius*, by Emil Schneweis.
30. Brian Hebblethwaite, *The Christian Hope* (Grand Rapids: William B. Eerdmans Publishing Company, 1984), 61.
31. Jaroslav Pelikan, *The Christian Tradition: A History of the Development of Doctrine*, vol. 3, *The Growth of Medieval Theology (600-1300)* (Chicago: Chicago University Press, 1978), 293-294.
32. Pelikan, 3:295.
33. Reginald Garrigou-Lagrange, *The Trinity and God the Creator: A Commentary on St. Thomas' Theological Summa*, Ia, q. 27-119, trans. Frederic C. Eckhoff (London: B. Herder Book Co., 1952), 531-532.
34. Pelikan, 3:297-298.
35. Hagenbach, 1:475.
36. Pelikan, 3:269.
37. Landrum P. Leavell, *Angels, Angels, Angels* (Nashville: Broadman Press, 1973), 10.
38. Pelikan, 3:293.
39. Ewert H. Cousins, preface to *Angelic Spirituality: Medieval Perspectives on the Ways of Angels*, introduced and trans. by Steven Chase in *The Classics of Western Spirituality*, ed. Bernard McGinn (New York: Paulist Press, 2002), xx.
40. *Angelic Spirituality: Medieval Perspectives on the Ways of Angels*, introduced and trans. by Steven Chase in the *The Classics of Western Spirituality*, ed. Bernard McGinn (New York: Paulist Press, 2002), 107.
41. *Angelic Spirituality*, 108.
42. For more information on the subject of angelic spirituality in the Middle Ages please see the second section of *Angelic Spirituality: Medieval Perspecitves on the Ways of Angels*, intro. and trans. by Steven Chase.

43. Hagenbach, 2:341.
44. Jaroslav Pelikan, *The Christian Tradition: A History of the Development of Doctrine*, vol. 4, *Reformation of Church and Dogma (1300-1700)* (Chicago: The University of Chicago Press, 1984), 336.
45. Martin Chemnitz, *Loci Theologici*, vol. 1, trans. J.A.O. Preus (St. Louis: Concordia Publishing House, 1989), 173.
46. Julius Kostlin, *The Theology of Luther in its Historical Development and Inner Harmony*, vol. 2, trans. Charles E. Hay (Philadelphia: Luther Publication Society, 1897; reprint in Concordia Heritage Series, St. Louis: Concordia Publishing House, 1986), 324-326 (page citations are to the reprint edition).
47. Chemnitz, 165.
48. Chemnitz, 165, 173-174.
49. Chemnitz, 165, 174.
50. Chemnitz, 165, 174.
51. This is probably why Luther included petitions regarding angelic protection in both his Morning and Evening Prayers.
52. Martin Luther, "The Day of St. Michael and All Angels: First Sermon, 1532," in *Sermons of Martin Luther: The House Postils*, ed. Eugene F. A. Klug, trans. Eugene F.A. Klug, et al, vol. 3, *Sermons on Gospel Texts for the Fifteenth through Twenty-Sixth Sundays after Trinity, the Festival of Christ's Nativity, and Other Occasions* (Grand Rapids: Baker Books, 1996), 375-376.
53. Luther, "First Sermon, 1532," 377.
54. Luther, "First Sermon, 1532," 378-380.
55. Martin Luther, "The Day of St. Michael and All Angels: Second Sermon, 1534," in *Sermons of Martin Luther: The House Postils*, ed. Eugene F. A. Klug, trans. Eugene F.A. Klug, et al., vol. 3, *Sermons on Gospel Texts for the Fifteenth through Twenty-Sixth Sundays after Trinity, the Festival of Christ's Nativity, and Other Occasions* (Grand Rapids: Baker Books, 1996), 387-388.
56. Luther, "Second Sermon, 1534," 389.
57. Kostlin, 326.
58. Martin Luther, "Lectures on Zechariah: The Latin Text" (1526), trans. Richard J. Dinda, in *Luther's Works*, ed. Hilton C. Oswald, vol. 20, *Lectures on the Minor Prophets III: Zechariah* (St. Louis: Concordia Publishing House, 1973), 117.
59. Kostlin, 326-327.
60. Chemnitz, 175-177.
61. Chemnitz, 177-178.
62. Justo L. Gonzalez, *A History of Christian Thought*, vol. 3, revised ed., *From the Protestant Reformation to the Twentieth Century* (Nashville: Abingdon Press, 1975), 140-141.
63. Gonzalez, 3:141.
64. Gonzalez, 3:141.
65. Hagenbach, 2:341.
66. For a more comprehensive look at Reformation angelology please see Martin Chemnitz's *Loci Theologici* or *A History of Christian Thought*, vol. 3, by Justo L. Gonzalez.
67. Hagenbach, 2:482.
68. Hagenbach, 2:482.
69. *A Treatise on Angel Magic: Being a Complete Transcription of Ms. Harley 6482 in the British Library*, ed. and intro. by Adam McLean, in the *Magnum Opus Hermetic Sourceworks #15*

(Grand Rapids: Phanes Press, 1990), 9.
70. *A Treatise on Angel Magic*, 12-13.
71. *A Treatise on Angel Magic*, 13.
72. *A Treatise on Angel Magic*, 180.
73. *A Treatise on Angel Magic*, 180-181.
74. *A Treatise on Angel Magic*, 182.
75. Friedrich Schleiermacher, *The Christian Faith*, ed. H.R. Mackintosh and J.S. Stewart (Edinburgh: T & T Clart, Ltd., 1999), 160.
76. Schleiermacher, 159.
77. Schleiermacher, 159, 161.
78. Schleiermacher, 159.
79. Alexander Whyte, "The Nature of Angels (I): December 18, 1870; St. George's, Edinburgh," in *The Nature of Angels: Eight Addresses by Alexander Whyte* (Grand Rapids: Baker Book House, 1930; reprinted 1976), 113.
80. Edward W.A. Koehler, *A Summary of Christian Doctrine: A Popular Presentation of the Teachings of the Bible* (Detroit: Louis H. Koehler, 1939; second revised edition, Oakland: Alfred W. Koehler, 1952), 44 (page citations are to the reprint edition).
81. Koehler, 44-45.
82. Koehler, 46-47.
83. Hope MacDonald, *When Angels Appear* (Grand Rapids: Daybreak Books, 1982), 13.
84. Gerhard Tersteegen, "God Himself is Present," in *Lutheran Worship*, prepared by the Commission on Worship of the Lutheran Church—Missouri Synod (St. Louis: Concordia Publishing House, 1982), #206.

2

Angels, Angels, Everywhere

Satan himself masquerades as an angel of light.
(2 Corinthians 11:14)

CURRENT TRENDS IN CONTEMPORARY WESTERN ANGELOLOGY

It is fascinating how rapidly the public's preoccupation with angels has changed. Just a few short decades ago, many people were hesitant to believe in angels at all.[1] Now, however, as the world enters the twenty-first century, angels are in the forefront of people's minds. They are used as marketing gimmicks to sell anything from tires to cream cheese. Roughly thirty years ago, one was hard-pressed to discover any information regarding angels in a public bookstore. Now, the section on angels usually dominates the religion section of major bookstore chains.[2] One is also subjected to a literal information overload upon entering a search for "angels" into an internet search engine ("angels" = 98,300,000; "angelology" = 165,000; "angel magic" = 109,000 websites).[3] This chapter will examine why this sudden shift has occurred and what types of angelology are now being presented for public consumption. As Eileen Freeman writes, "In the wake of people's interest in angels and hunger for more information about them and how to be in touch with them, we are now seeing some goods and 'services' being offered that go beyond mere foolishness and wind up in the realm of pure quackery—or worse."[4]

THE EFFECTS OF POSTMODERNISM ON ANGELOLOGY

As stated in the previous chapter, modernism sought to answer life's questions through reason. The spirit realm was easily discounted because one could not subject it to scientific testing. "The modern era employed the scientific method and rationalism reigned supreme. The rational mind brought people to the truth, and science was believed to possess the answers."[5] In making these assumptions, the modern era enjoyed thinking virtually everything was explainable.[6]

However, the western world has recently entered a new era, known as the postmodern era. "Postmodern" is an actual era of time [ca. 1970 to the present]. "Postmodernism" is a belief system or philosophy held by postmodernists or postmoderns.[7] The postmodern era has emerged in reaction to the failure of the modern period to solve humanity's problems. This era no longer holds up rationalism, reason, and science as the ultimate judges of truth. "This postmodern culture is thoroughly post-scientific, believing in the supernatural and very aware of activity in the spiritual realm."[8]

In this cultural shift, "the intellect is replaced by the will. Reason is replaced by emotion. Morality is replaced by relativism. Reality itself becomes a social contract."[9]

A major component of this new culture is experience. The "old" modern need for explanation has been replaced in postmodernism with a thirst for experience. Indeed, this emerging culture cannot be fully appreciated without understanding the drive for experience within this society. Postmoderns have a need to experience things for themselves.[10] They "do not so much want to hear about God as they desire to hear from God."[11]

Due to the stress which postmoderns place upon the vitality of experience in their spiritual lives, they do not need to be convinced of the miraculous. Indeed, they already believe in the unseen, and they wish for contact with the supernatural. However, they do not desire to discover meaning, but their purpose in life, through these contacts.[12] As Leonard Sweet points out, "postmoderns are constantly putting their hands and the rest of their bodies as well where God may have visited, hoping it's still warm. They are hungry for experiences, especially experiences of God."[13] While this push towards personal experiences of God has made postmoderns open to the spiritual realm, it has also done much harm to the Biblical doctrine of objective truth. "Modernists did not believe the Bible is true. Postmodernists have cast out the category of truth altogether. In doing so, they have opened up a Pandora's box of New Age religions, syncretism, and moral chaos."[14] One's personal experience, not an "outside" source (i.e. the Bible), is now determinative of truth.

In his book *Angels and the New Spirituality*, Duane Garrett provides a clear link between postmodernism and the New Age Movement. "The postmodern society wants spirituality, significance, belonging, and consolation against the impersonal nature of modern life. It frankly does not care how outlandish or irrational the answer might be so long as it fills this need."[15] While the New Age Movement is not easy to describe or define, it is a grassroots movement that has no leadership to establish an agenda. Though New Age followers do not adhere fully to any authoritative Scripture such as the Bible, Koran, or the Book of Mormon, they are pluralistic and syncretistic, fusing these and many other religious texts as well.[16]

Indeed, one of the frustrations in discussing the subject of postmodern New Age thinking is its extreme lack of cohesion. This is especially true in the realm of angelology. New Age angelology does not distinguish one source from another in terms of credibility—the Bible, the Koran, Emmanuel Swedenborg's writings, and many other works are all seen as equal. There is no objective truth.[17] "They make little or no effort to reconcile contradictions in how these diverse sources understood angels. Doctrinal inconsistency does not bother them. Rather, they want to build a case that angels are everywhere and talk to all kinds of people with all kinds of religious backgrounds."[18] The emphasis of New Age angelology has nothing to do with doctrine, but with the belief that anyone can initiate communication with angels, though the methodology for establishing contact varies widely.[19]

Above all, postmoderns desire a deeply spiritual life. Though they quickly reject the Christian God of their fathers, they now embrace the spirituality of the East, the occult, and the gods and goddesses of the ancient world. They have embraced these appealing forms of spirituality in order to fill the vacuum in their lives left behind by rationalistic modernism.[20] This blended form of New Age spirituality has become so popular among people today that it has become pervasive throughout western society. "Its vision of the supernatural world has achieved a fairly complete victory over traditional

Christian teachings in movies and television. And it has now entered the realm of the angels."[21] The following discussion will focus on some of the many beliefs regarding the nature and function of angels espoused by the New Age Movement.

PROFILES OF ANGELIC NATURE

It is important to remember that each author has a different slant regarding the nature of angels. Therefore, there are many diverse published beliefs regarding the nature of angels. However, due to the overwhelming number of beliefs, only a select few will be discussed. Some authors come very close to the Christian viewpoint and see angels as created spiritual beings, subject to God.[22] However, the Biblical witness is rarely, if ever, allowed to stand on its own. As is the case with much New Age spiritism, beliefs regarding the nature of angels are invariably linked with the angelologies of various other religious bodies. This is because the "idea of spirits mediating between gods and mortals is a part of almost every traditional belief system that we know of. It is as old as the gods themselves. Nearly all the great religions have preserved this tradition in their teachings."[23]

Francis Melville goes on to suggest that the different traditions of Judaism, Christianity, and Islam have been influenced by ancient Hinduism and Buddhism.[24] Or one might view angels from a Jungian perspective, which stresses that angels are powerful psychological archetypes. There is very little cohesion even within a single author's perspective because, following postmodern and New Age thinking, "in the end it is the individual heart, not the rational mind, that establishes a relationship with angels."[25] Therefore, one may believe practically anything; it is the act of belief that matters most. As Paul Roland writes, "you do not have to be a 'religious' person to appeal for help from the angels. Nor do you have to subscribe to a specific belief system, other than the belief which says that as a Divine being you have the right to ask for assistance from those who serve the universal life force, and you have the right to expect their help."[26]

Concerning the creation of angels, Sophy Burnham presents yet more conflicting views. At one point she notes that they are winged spirits. However, the closer they come to God the less form they have; they are pure energy and are only depicted symbolically.[27] Though angels have existed from the beginning of time they have changed during time both in nature and in function. The earliest angels had no wings and did not fly.[28] Indeed, this belief that angels have evolved over time is also upheld by Paul Roland when he writes that "angels cannot possibly be inert, limited to one stage of evolution, or ranked in a static hierarchy, when everything else in creation is constantly evolving, striving consciously or instinctively toward its ultimate potential."[29]

Angels are also believed to be able to appear in all shapes, sizes, and colours, visible or invisible to the human eye. They may even impersonate people that one knows. It is also said that angels come as thoughts, visions, dreams, animals, light on the water or in the clouds, rainbows, as well as people. They are described as being pure thoughts, which Burnham equates with *sudden* knowledge or *sudden* insight. If one has a good idea or brilliant inspiration, it most assuredly came not from the person, but from an angel.[30]

The idea that angels are pure thought forms may account for why Burnham says that there is nothing one can know for certain about angels. People are only given fleeting glimpses in their hearts.[31] This in turn makes it very easy for people to believe whatever they desire because whatever angelic experience each of them has in their heart is true for each of them, since there is no objective truth from which to test their experiences. This line of thinking is intricately tied to the above discussion, stressing again the postmodern belief in personal experience as the guide to ultimate truth. Angelic experiences are "real" for the people who experience them; this gives them great authority. Indeed, the belief in angels is not so much based on any outside source (such as the Bible, which cannot be trusted), but on a person's past experiences.[32]

In the early part of his book Roland has a disclaimer stating "what follows is my personal interpretation of the invisible realms and their inhabitants as passed down to me by my teachers and filtered through revelation and personal experience. Each reader should weigh the truth of what follows for themselves and accept only what feels right for them," in accordance with esoteric tradition.[33] This direction, however, does not apply to people who would hold to a traditional Biblical account of angels. These he treats with derision and scorn. Roland holds that those who view angels merely as "divine messengers" are grossly misinformed. This view limits their understanding of the nature and purpose of existence by imposing human values on what is beyond human comprehension.[34] Indeed, in contrast to his strong foundation of personal experience (which he states can be taken or left at one's discretion), Roland contends that much of Christian angelology is pure supposition and speculation.[35]

Intricately tied to the nature of angels is a person's belief regarding his or her own existence. If one is a lowly human being created by a Higher Power, then angels are also created beings, that is external beings apart from humans. However, John Price writes:

> The universe is a macrocosm of creative energy and power, and every man, woman, and child is the epitome of this totality of the cosmos. Within your individualized energy field, the microcosm called you, are twenty-two Causal Powers, or angels, that control your conscious behaviour and govern the manifestations of all forms and experiences in your personal life. Their existence has been taught since the beginning of spiritual brotherhoods and philosophical societies thousands of years ago.[36]

Angels are popularly viewed as a manifestation of thought originating from within oneself. As such, they may be controlled by a person, as long as that person recognizes his or her own divinity. As Price writes, "they are divine thoughtforms operating under the Law of Free Will, which means that they are subject to the energy that we are consciously or unconsciously radiating."[37] Roland, along with his many other ideas concerning angelic nature, also holds that angels are forms of thought. Indeed, he stresses that one can create an angelic thought form to provide oneself with protection, and he even provides examples of rituals (spells) to use.[38] In fact, Roland goes so far as to say that there is a very powerful angel within each person; a Holy Guardian Angel, which gives a person divine guidance and power. The person and his or her Guardian Angel are actually one and the same. They only seem to be two separate entities because human perception is usually too limited to be able to grasp more than one reality at a time.[39]

There is also a general belief that ghosts are not angels. However, some people believe that angels are the deified souls of departed spirits, because human souls evolve into higher forms, angels being one of those forms.[40] The beliefs concerning angelic nature are many and diverse. However, most New Age writers agree that angels are good, and radiate warmth, peace, and well-being.[41] True angelic nature represents all that is good, true, and beautiful (but may be defiled by one's ego, in which case a person will no longer experience those optimal qualities in his or her life). Indeed, because their nature is intricately tied together with their function, it is the angel's duty to emit the true nature of its being, which consists of success, harmony, loving relationships, abundance, or whatever else its specific assignment might be. And because the angel's primary task is to serve human beings, individuals may override its primary nature and create a different assignment for it to follow.[42]

Linked with the idea of the innate "goodness" of angels is the common belief that Satan and evil angels do not really exist. Evil spirits are either the spirits of disturbed human beings, or products of the human mind. Devils are merely figments of human imagination and projections of personal guilt and fear. People make their own demons. There is really no such thing as evil, for what people perceive as evil acts are merely bad acts of fellow human beings, which only occur because those people are not conscious of their divine nature. "Evil is the lack of conscience caused by separation from the source."[43] Therefore, Price asserts, if one has problems, they are due to one's own projection of false images onto one's personal living energies (angels), which in turn replicate and project these falsities onto the outer screen of the phenomenal world (human perception of reality), and they will continue to project these negative appearances until the energy of manifestation (which is rooted in one's own consciousness) is changed.[44]

However, once more the lack of cohesion (which occurs both among different writers and within individual writers) quickly becomes evident, as Burnham adamantly holds that demons and evil do exist. Demons lie and make people think that there is no order in the universe beyond one's pain and fear. However, she does not believe in a personal hell where people are punished after death. She believes that people make their own hells here on earth, in their minds and hearts. Angels, she asserts, help us to escape from this condition.[45]

However, most books on the subject are simply dismissive of the demonic. Some believe that evil spirits may exist, but that they can easily be avoided, either by ignoring them or telling them to go away.[46] Others such as Price believe that Satan has been given a bad reputation by fundamentalist religious groups like Christianity. Noting that Satan is the Angel of Materiality and Temptation, a holy helper, he declares:

> We are from the fourth dimension, and the major part of our being has remained on that level, with our mental, emotional, and physical bodies extended into the third dimension. Our objective is to enjoy the physical-plane experience without getting trapped in the fog of materiality. This means that we are to "live, love, laugh, and be happy" without the emotional bondage of fear, guilt, greed, and sorrow. Our role in this world is to have everything without possessing anything — to enjoy an all-sufficiency of money without being preoccupied with "making money," to have right livelihood without toiling to make a living, to have wholeness without focussing on the body, to have right relations without selfish emotional affections.[47]

During one of his conversations with Satan, Price was told:

> Live for the fun of it, and die for the fun of it. Nothing else really matters.
>
> Play more, for the fun of it; love and make love more, for the fun of it. Touch and hold and kiss the one who lights up your life, for the fun of it. Why look back with any regrets?
>
> Laugh and giggle and sing and dance, for the fun of it, as a little child without a care, for truly there is no tomorrow, only today.
>
> Be unconventional and nonconforming, a little crazy, for the fun of it. Be a gleeful self and see a hilarious world, for the fun of it. Regardless of what may happen, it will happen, for the fun of it.
>
> Trust the Presence and Power of God [that is one's Higher Self], for the fun of it. Surrender to the activity of God in every aspect of life, for the fun of it.
>
> Do everything in life just for the fun of it. Nothing else really matters.[48]

Price holds that one should contact and converse with this Causal Power as one would with any special friend. It is important to remember that Satan "functions as an 'alarm system' to keep your head in the spiritual realm while your feet are in the gentle surf of delightful experiences on the physical plane. As you learn from his tests, you will be protected from wading too far out into the drowning waters of materialism and will be lifted toward the Holy Mountain."[49] Along with Garret, "I cannot but wonder if New Age angelphiles [those obsessed with contacting angels] have made too many special friends of this kind."[50]

Most of the current popular books do not have much to say about the nature and creation of angels. They are much more concerned with what angels do (their function and purpose) and how they may be used to serve humanity. Often, they merely affirm angelic existence and then move on to relating how one may know and communicate with one's special angels. After stating that angels are simply messengers of the divine realm, Albert Haldane and Simha Seraya write in their book *Angel Signs*, that "your Angelscope [their guide which relates a special guardian angel for each five-day segment of the year] will reveal how you can learn more about yourself, deepen your spirituality, enrich your life, and enhance your talents (talents you never knew you had) by making your guardian angel a special part of your daily life."[51]

PROFILES OF ANGELIC FUNCTIONS

From the Christian perspective, the methods used by non-Christians for contacting angels are a cause for unease and even alarm. Some of the methods described by various authors for contacting angels will be discussed and some will be reproduced in full detail in the appendices at the end of this study. Christians see such methods as being contrary to God's Word, and even making one susceptible to evil spirits. Christians believe that "your enemy the devil prowls around like a roaring lion looking for someone to devour," (1 Peter 5:8) and are forbidden to attempt contact with spirits (Leviticus 19:26; Deuteronomy 18:10-11).

Among New Age angelphiles there is a profound belief that angels are everywhere and do everything, and that there is a specific angel for every purpose. Angels have the power to help people transform their lives because angels are gods/goddesses, just given different names.[52] Angels are always ready and willing to intervene and provide assistance for people; all one needs to do is ask them for their help (though they may be unable to help at times due to a person's bad karma).[53] People require assistance from angels because angels "are the living Governors of Life, each controlling a Gate, or opening, leading to the phenomenal world—conditioning and determining all outer expression."[54] Angels may also rescue people, give people aid, anoint people with calm and serenity, deliver messages of warning or hope, guide people, teach people, answer people's prayers, and lead them to death.[55] The goal for every human being is to become perfect in his or her life. In order to do this one must garner the help of angels, which is facilitated by giving love and adoration to the angel within.[56]

In order to properly gain an angel's help, one must first properly contact the angel. Again, the methods for this contact vary widely with each individual author. Some promote meditation techniques (invocation), whereas others offer actual spells and incantations or evocations to summon one's guardian angel. All of these practices fall under the realm of the popular phrase "angel magic." Evocations are spells that use various tools to invoke the physical appearance or manifestation of a specific angel. Invocations, while similar in nature to evocations, have one big difference. Through an invocation, a person is attempting to summon the angel within his or her own body to establish communication with a spiritual being. From a Christian perspective this is far more dangerous than evocations, yet invocation is considered much easier to do and is promoted more often.[57]

As previously stated, the most frequently espoused method for making contact with angels is meditation. Roland believes that people should establish contact with each of the seven angels that are said to govern the chakras (subtle energy centres in the human body). By contacting them daily, preferably before breakfast and bed, one will release vital energy which will balance, ground, and protect him or her from negativity.[58] To aid those unable to successfully meditate by themselves in their pursuit of becoming attuned with their inner (eternal) self, there are Angelic Chakra Readings available on the internet. For a nominal fee of $20.00, the user may ask three questions from a professional "diviner" regarding the estate of their seven chakras. In these readings the angels "speak" from their hearts and "sing" their words of wisdom to the individual. These readings provide the individual with the opportunity to "hear" those messages that ring true to his or her inner and intuitive self.[59]

These meditations take on various forms, depending on the author. However, they frequently involve such things as relaxation techniques, self-examination, release of all negativity, coming into closer alignment with the outside world, and finally, conversing with one's angel.[60] "Simply stated, these books advocate that we contact angels by working through our negative emotions, entering a meditative state, opening our minds to an angel encounter, and then engaging in an imaginary meeting in which we hold a conversation with an angel in our own mind."[61] However, the method varies depending upon what kind of angel one wishes to encounter. Roland has different exercises to use to contact different angels: from the angel of forgiveness to the angel of water and the angel of the inner temple.[62] Price also has differing suggested meditations for all of his twenty-two angels, from the angel of unconditional love and reality to the angel of materiality and temptation.[63] To look more closely at examples of these meditations, refer to appendix B.

In Albert Haldane and Simha Seraya's book, *Angel Signs*, invocations are provided for each Angelscope. The authors recommend that, before one invokes his or her angel, he/she consider the request, focus upon the inner intentions behind the request, make sure the intention relates primarily to him/herself, open a channel between earth and the infinite by focussing inward, watch and listen carefully for an answer, and always express gratitude.[64] To properly perform the invocation one must say the angel's name properly, using the phonetic key provided, get in tune with the universal resonance, and align oneself with the angel's specific colour harmonization, which is also provided.[65] For more on this method refer to appendix B.

The second method used for making angel contact is evocation. "An evocation differs from an invocation or a petition in that it embodies a request, or a summons, for a specific spirit to manifest before us instead of simply an address to an angel."[66] The performer is warned that these rituals are to be undertaken with great care as angels are powerful manifestations of psychic energy that can possibly damage the mind of the unwary, undisciplined, or uneducated. One should not attempt these spells until one has become familiar with invocations and petitions, made contact with his or her guardian angel, and familiarized oneself with the various energetic qualities of the angel to be evoked. One should know the ritual so well, prior to performing it, that one can visualize the entire ritual with one's eyes shut. If one is confident and has brought forth powerful contained energy, the evocation should be successful. If one has failed, the person should try again.[67] For a specific evocation ritual, refer to appendix C.

What is readily apparent upon closer examination of these rituals is that they strongly advocate idol worship as well as sorcery. They foster idol worship in the sense of praying to and receiving guidance from the spirits one contacts,[68] activities which are supposed to be reserved for God alone. However, this traditional limitation may be circumvented by referring to oneself as god (or God-Self), as Price regularly does in his meditations.[69] Therefore, it becomes normal and acceptable to pray to oneself for forgiveness and better understanding—with the help of one's guiding angel, of course. These ideas should seem strange to Christians and certainly serve as warning signs that what is being advocated is unsafe and contrary to God's will, and yet Christians are still being drawn into this dangerous belief system. This is because it is commonplace for New Age angelology writers to use much Christian terminology to put the reader's mind at ease.[70] This causes confusion and can lead Christians to inadvertently go against God's Word.

Sorcery is also frequently referred to and used in these books, which commonly use the phrase "angel magic." Angel magic is used to establish contact with one's angel in order to garner information[71] or to become a better person.[72] It is obvious, however, that whether it be magic or prayer, the rituals involved in contacting angels take power away from God and give it to His created creatures. God becomes no longer necessary (unless it is the god within or an angelic god), as these mediators have the power to grant one's every desire.[73] This is a very self-centred system which advocates manipulation in order to gain power over one's life at the expense of the Author and Perfector of all life.

It is interesting that no matter whether the ritual is invocation or evocation, knowing the name of the angel is extremely important. Though names may differ and change over time, it is the process of naming that makes a difference. Garrett surmises that this is because giving angels names makes them seem more authentic and personal, which makes it easier to convince people that angels are real. Also, if one attaches a name to an angel, it appears that one knows that angel well. Those who know their angels can do no wrong.[74]

Garrett views these exercises as vain and silly. They will not free a person from fear, guilt, or lust. However, from a Christian perspective, they are not without a deeper, more dangerous, purpose. They lead people into lowering their spiritual defences, which then allows alien spiritual powers to enter. This is extremely dangerous because, though these people are frequently opening themselves up to the spirit world in this way, they are very often naïve with respect to evil spirits. Often, they believe that simply telling an evil spirit (if they even believe that evil spirits exist) to stay away will compel it to do so.[75] This author believes it may not, and it could even open the door to possession.

This is the backdrop for the plethora of views that are currently popular in contemporary western culture regarding angelic nature and function. Angels are viewed as spiritual beings that can aid the believer in attaining a higher understanding of one's divine self. The various ideas that have arisen from the New Age spiritual climate of the postmodern era are in contrast to the Scriptural perspective. It is the task of the church to provide Biblically-based answers to the many people in society who wish to learn more about angels and their meaning for the individual person, and to give warning.

> *Though hordes of devils fill the land all threat'ning to devour us,*
> *We tremble not, unmoved we stand; They cannot overpow'r us.*
> *Let this world's tyrant rage; in battle we'll engage.*
> *His might is doomed to fail; God's judgement must prevail!*
> *One little word subdues him.*[76]

Chapter Notes: Chapter 2

1. Claus Westermann, *God's Angels Need No Wings*, trans. David L. Scheidt (Philadelphia: Fortress Press, 1979), 12.

2. Duane A. Garrett, *Angels and the New Spirituality* (Nashville: Broadman & Holman Publishers, 1995), 131.

3. Google Search, "Angels" (world wide web page) http://www.google.ca/#hl=en&source=hp&q=angels&aq=f&aqi=g10&aql=&oq=&gs_rfai=&fp=9c397ca33127ba2d [June 8, 2010]; Google Search, "Angelology" (world wide web page)http://www.google.ca/#hl=en&q=angelology&aq=f&aqi=g10&aql=&oq=&gs_rfai=&fp=9c397ca33127ba2d [June 8, 2010]; Google Search, "Angel Magic" (world wide web page) http://www.google.ca/#hl=en&q=%22angel+magic%22&aq=f&aqi=g6g-m2g-ms1g-m1&aql=&oq=&gs_rfai=&fp=9c397ca33127ba2d [June 8, 2010].

4. Eileen Elias Freeman, *Angelic Healing: Working with Your Angels to Heal Your Life* (New York: Warner Books, 1994), xi.
5. Matt Ziprick, "The Gospel for a Postmodern Culture" (M. Div. Thesis, Concordia Lutheran Seminary, Edmonton, AB, 2002), 9.
6. Ziprick, 16.
7. Gene Edward Veith, Jr., *Postmodern Times: A Christian Guide to Contemporary Thought and Culture in Turning Point Christian Worldview Series*, ed. Marvin Olasky (Wheaton: Crossway Books, 1994), 42.
8. Ziprick, 1.
9. Veith, 29.
10. Ziprick, 3-4.
11. Ziprick, 4.
12. Leonard Sweet, *Soul Tsunami* (Grand Rapids: Zondervan, 1999), 208.
13. Leonard Sweet, *Postmodern Pilgrims* (Nashville: Broadman& Holman Publishers, 2000), 49.
14. Veith, 192-193.
15. Garrett, 128.
16. Garrett, 127.
17. Garrett, 131-132.
18. Garrett, 132.
19. Garrett, 141.
20. Garrett, 128.
21. Garrett, 131
22. Freeman, 27.
23. Francis Melville, *The Book of Angels* (Hauppage: Barron's Educational Series Inc., 2001), 6.
24. Melville, 7.
25. Melville, 8.
26. Paul Roland, *Angels: A Piatkus Guide* (London: Judy Piatkus Publishers, Ltd., 1999), 5-6.
27. Sophy Burnham, *A Book of Angels: Reflections on Angels Past and Present and True Stories of How They Touch Our Lives* (New York: Ballantine Books, 1990), 19, 21.
28. Burnham, 82, 87.
29. Roland, 32.
30. Burnham, 29, 40, 56.
31. Burnham, 21-22.
32. Roland, 1, 3.
33. Roland, 6.
34. Roland, 1.
35. Roland, 17.
36. John Randolph Price, *The Angels Within Us: A Spiritual Guide to the Twenty-Two Angels that Govern Our Lives* (New York: Fawcett Columbine, 1993), 9.
37. Price, 12.
38. Roland, 64.
39. Roland, 104, 108.

40. Burnham, 17, 128.
41. Roland, 42.
42. Price, 13.
43. Roland, 63.
44. Price, 13.
45. Burnham, 150, 158.
46. Garrett, 160.
47. Price, 213.
48. Price, 209-210.
49. Price, 217.
50. Garrett, 160.
51. Albert Haldane and Simha Seraya with Barbara Lagowski, *Angel Signs: A Celestial Guide to the Powers of Your Own Guardian Angel* (New York: HarperSanFrancisco, 2002), 3.
52. Garrett, 151-152.
53. Roland, 3, 46.
54. Price, 10.
55. Burnham, 45.
56. Price, 16.
57. Karyn Easton, "Angel Magic" (world wide web page) http://www.paranormality.com/angel_magic.shtml [3 March 2003].
58. Roland, 7-8.
59. Kimba, "Angelic Divination Readings" (world wide web page) http://kimbasangels.com/angelreadings.html [3 March 2003].
60. Garrett, 142-144.
61. Garrett, 145.
62. Roland, 75-77, 89-91, 104-107.
63. Price, 29-31, 217-218.
64. Haldane and Seraya, 6-8.
65. Haldane and Seraya, 4-6.
66. Melville, 122.
67. Melville, 122-123.
68. Burnham, 45.
69. Price, 218.
70. Garrett, 142.
71. Roland, 51-52.
72. Price, 16.
73. Roland, 5-6, 104, 108.
74. Garrett, 133, 138.
75. Garrett, 144, 147.
76. Martin Luther, "A Mighty Fortress Is Our God."

Angelic Nature and Function

A Scriptural Perspective

*There is rejoicing in the presence of the angels
of God over one sinner who repents.
(Luke 15:10)*

In the previous chapter it was shown that there are many diverse and strange ideas held by many people today concerning angels. "In view of this rising tide of demonism, spiritism, astrology, and fortune-telling, a study of angels takes on greater importance."[1] Also, Robert Jenson notes there are many people today who advocate "creation spirituality" (worshiping creation) which, according to Scripture, is idolatry (Deuteronomy 17:2-5). Humanity holds the universe's beauty and majesty in awe. It is simply sinful human nature for human beings to enact this awe and dependence religiously. Some people worship and sacrifice to the elements; others pray to animal spirits, and still others worship the stars, sun, and moon. However, humanity's relation to other creatures is not to change. Galaxies, aardvarks, and angels are all creatures and are not to be worshiped. They are not gods or demigods, and the one true God commands humanity not to place faith in or give worship to any god but Him[2] (Exodus 20:3-5).

In light of this rampant idolatry and great interest in angels, it is imperative for the church to have ready responses based upon the teachings of Holy Scripture. Though one may be saved without knowledge of angels, it is a grievous sin to knowingly reject (or distort) this doctrine as it is plainly taught in Scripture.[3] It is the task of the Christian, therefore, to speak plainly and clearly against any false belief that may arise about the nature and function of God's heavenly creatures. This chapter will outline the teachings of Scripture in this regard.

THE BIBLICAL UNDERSTANDING OF ANGELS

First, the question of the creation of angels must be discussed. Scripture clearly teaches that angels do indeed exist. However, the Bible does not specify the time of their creation, though it certainly occurred within the first six days of creation. Angels could not have been created before the world because that would clearly contradict John 1:1-3, Colossians 1:16, and Genesis 1:1 to 2:1, which relate that all things (the heavens, the earth, and all creatures, including angels) were created through Jesus Christ within the first six days of creation. Nor is it possible that angels were created after the sixth day because on the seventh day God rested from His act of Creation, which He had completed according to Genesis 2:1-3.[4] Though some theologians place the time for the angels' creation on the first day, based upon Job 38:4-7, it may be best to conclude only that they were created within the first six days.[5]

Regardless of when they were created, it is clear that angels are part of the created order. Angels, along with humans and all other beings, are created, in contrast to the Creator. The Bible speaks of angels as being a part of the "heavenly" world which, nevertheless, was created. In Psalm 148 the psalmist speaks of all parts of creation praising God (sun, moon, and the angels).[6] As the psalmist says, "Praise Him, all His angels, praise Him, all His heavenly hosts….Let them praise the name of the Lord, for He commanded and they were created."[7] Indeed, though there is no specific

Confessional Article in the *Book of Concord* in which angels are considered, there are scattered references which yield important information.[8] For example, the Epitome to the Formula of Concord specifically refers to angels as beings created by God.[9]

The nature of angels is described with one word—spirit ($\pi\nu\varepsilon\hat{\upsilon}\mu\alpha$). Angels are spirits without bodily form.[10] Indeed, it has been revealed that "angels are not mere physical or moral forces, but distinct spiritual beings, which God created (Hebrews 1:14)."[11] Francis Pieper also holds that angels are spirits or immaterial beings. He further states, on the basis of Luke 24:39, that humans are forbidden to ascribe even an ethereal corporeity to angels, for a "spirit is the direct opposite (*oppositio adequate*) to every form of corporeity, including the glorified form."[12]

It is important to remember that while angels are spirit as God is spirit, they are vastly different from God. Angels are finite creatures whereas God is infinite.[13] However, it is also imperative to remember that "angels are not merely 'ideas' or 'impulses,' but spirits of real substance."[14] It is also probable that because angels are spirits and lack bodily form they are usually not visible to the physical eye. Paul, in Colossians 1:16, appears to equate "things in heaven" with the "invisible" things, which include principalities and powers, which are in turn often explained as angels. Though angels are primarily invisible to humans, they may yet appear bodily to relay messages from God to His people. Some Biblical examples of this occurring are found in Genesis 18:1-2, 19:1; Mark 16:5; and Matthew 28:2-7.[15] Lewis Sperry Chafer speculates that one reason angels may be rendered invisible to the human eye is because man would be so prone to worship them[16] (Revelation 22:8).

Hope MacDonald writes that angels are spiritual beings who cannot normally be seen, but are often very beautiful when they do become visible. They are personal beings who represent God but are not omnipresent as only God is. However, they sometimes do appear as humans and may, according to Hebrews 13:2, be mistaken as such.[17] It cannot be explained how angels ate food at times, any more than their assumption of an accidental body can be explained. However, their temporary consumption of food (Genesis 18) and assumption of a body served to convince the people to whom they appeared of their true presence. It is further affirmed in Scripture that although angels are spiritual and immaterial beings, they can and have acted upon the bodies of men (Genesis 19:16; Matthew 4:5).[18]

Being created spirits and dependent upon God, angels are immutable, not being subject to physical changes (i.e. they do not procreate, grow old, nor can they die although, like men, they have a beginning without an end).[19] Since they are immortal, their number will not decrease. Being spirits, with no body, they are sexless, and so neither will they increase in number.[20] Indeed, the total number of angels is unknown, though the Bible refers to them in many places, including Revelation 5:11, as numbering thousands upon thousands. However, the number of angels has remained constant since their very creation.[21] In fact, angels are so numerous that the "Fathers liked to explain the parable of the lost sheep by saying that the latter represented mankind and the ninety-nine the angels."[22] Yet it is impossible to compute accurately the number of angels with exactness. Suffice it to say that the number of angels is very large according to Daniel 7:10, Luke 2:13, and Hebrews 12:22.[23] Though their number is great, angels are not omnipresent, as is God. They are present in only one place at one time. However, they are not locally present, but illocally present, for "they do not occupy and fill a definite circumscribed space, where their presence could be felt."[24] Yet even as they serve God's people on earth, they behold the Father's face in heaven.[25]

Angels also possess agility or velocity. They are able to move about the universe, though not as a physical person.[26] In fact, they are able to move so quickly that they can come to people on earth with a message from God concerning a prayer that a person has not yet finished praying (Daniel 9:21).[27] Of course, this works both ways, as they are also said to carry our prayers to God (Revelation 8:3-4; Tobit 12:12).[28]

The Bible also speaks of angels as being intelligent creatures with great power. It is a power that is superior to human strength (2 Thessalonians 1:7; Psalm 91:11-13). However, this knowledge and power are limited. The angels are neither omnipotent nor omniscient. They do not know all things, and particularly they have no knowledge of future events. Nor do the angels know the thoughts of men, since this is a prerogative of God only (1 Kings 8:39). However, because angels are intelligent, they can form conjectural opinions based upon man's outward words and deeds.[29] The knowledge that angels have, they know only as creatures. Even so, they may know things by virtue of their peculiar nature (2 Samuel 14:20), which is natural knowledge; by divine revelation (1 Peter 1:12; Luke 2:9-12), which is revealed knowledge; and by the beatific vision[30] that they enjoy (Matthew 18:10), which is beatific knowledge.[31]

Though their power is great, it too is limited and subordinate to the power of the Almighty Creator (which holds true both for God's holy angels and for Satan and his fallen brood). Though the devils can at times perform deeds that appear to men as miracles, they cannot perform real miracles, for only God can do such wonderful things (Psalm 72:18).[32] Also, God's good angels can only perform miracles in the name of God, through His power.

Indeed, their power is finite and completely under God's control (Job 1:12).[33] This limitation on their power is also attested in the Confessions, which relate that no angel has authority to establish articles of faith. Only the Word of God has the power and authority to do that.[34]

All angels were created in the Truth (John 8:44), in holiness, in righteousness and in the image of God, which has to be restored in man (Ephesians 4:24).[35] All angels possess freedom of will and great power for service, for which they were designed. Being confirmed in their "bliss," their wills are now completely conformed to God's will and so they freely serve Him. They have free will with respect to internal acts such as choosing or rejecting (Jude 6), as well as external acts such as locomotion or praising God. Though all angels were equally created righteous, good, and holy, some chose to reject God and fell from a state of grace to a state of misery. Those who remained true to God were given, as a gracious reward for their obedience, confirmation in their goodness so that they may no longer lose their goodness and become evil. They forever behold God in holy service having passed from a state of grace into a state of glory (Matthew 18:10; 1 Timothy 5:21; Luke 20:36; and Galatians 1:8). While they enjoy the beatific vision, they can no longer sin, nor do they desire to sin (2 Corinthians 11:14). They still possess free will, but it is directed only to that which is holy (Revelation 14:10).[36]

The evil angels, however, turned away from God of their own free will (Jude 6) and will forever be tormented without hope of returning to God.[37] The evil angels are not merely a personification of evil in the world or in man, but are also personal spiritual beings. They sinned, not because of any defect in their original nature, "but in full possession of their intellect, with deliberate design, and voluntary abuse of their will."[38] Though originally created good and holy, they sinned (2 Peter 2:4); following Satan who had made a beginning of sin (1 John 3:8) in rejecting the truth (John 8:44), they lost their first estate (which was good and holy) and left their heavenly abode (Jude 6).[39]

These evil angels are now forever rejected. There is no redemption for them because Christ came to save man, not angels. Their nature has been perverted. They are now deceitful (Genesis 3:1), murderers (John 8:44), and utterly depraved and wicked (Mark 1:23; Ephesians 6:12). There are many of them and they are powerful. God has permitted these evil spirits to roam the earth until the final Day of Judgement. However, these wicked spirits are forever subject to God's authority and power. They cannot go further than He permits (Job 1:12, 2:6). Nor shall they ever prevail against the church (Matthew 16:18; Romans 16:20). They have no choice but to serve God's purposes and adhere to His will in terms of chastening the faithful and punishing the wicked (Psalm 78:49).[40]

THE BIBLICAL FUNCTION OF ANGELS

It is very important to remember that the terms for angel (מַלְאָךְ, ἄγγελος) are not descriptive of those beings' essence, but of their office, signifying "one sent," or a messenger.[41] There are numerous examples throughout the Bible of angels delivering God's messages. Sometimes the message is one of God's love and deliverance (Luke 1:12-13, 30, 2:10; Matthew 28:5), whereas at other times it is indicative of divine judgement and anger against those who have defied the Lord (Genesis 19:1, 11; 2 Samuel 24:15-17; Acts 12:23). However, even as He does not send His angels to frighten His people (their repeated message to people being, "Fear not!"), so also His divine judgement and mercy are intended to bring His people back into a right relationship with Him. When people do repent, the promise of Luke 15:10 is fulfilled and people may continue in their walk of life confident that their loving God is by their side (Isaiah 43:1).[42]

Primarily, however, angels are responsible only to God, and obey only His commands. Indeed, their primary task is to serve God through worship and praise (Psalm 103:20, 148:2; Hebrews 1:6).[43] They are His ministers to do His pleasure, listening to the voice of His Word (Psalm 103:21).[44] As Chafer points out, their most important service is rendered not to humans but to God. Their worship of God began at their creation and will never cease.[45] The Confessions hold that the holy angels give to God total and spontaneous obedience in all things, of their own free will.[46]

As the angels in heaven worship God and render Him honour as their primary duty, so also humanity should do likewise. Therefore, since people are only to serve and worship God, it follows that they must always avoid worshiping angels (Revelation 22:8-9). People should not pray to angels, though it is permissible and right to pray to God to send His helping angels to someone; there is no Scriptural warrant to ask the angels directly.[47] Indeed, though angels are to be highly esteemed as God's blessed messengers, and people are to rejoice in their ministry and regard them with pious awe, angels are not to worshiped, since they too are creatures.[48]

In response, therefore, to the advice often espoused in popular books concerning how to contact one's own angel, the biblical view is, "Forget about getting in touch with an angel—get in touch with God! Don't ask angels to do anything—ask God!"[49] Christians must hold firm to the conviction that though angels in heaven may pray for humanity, it does not necessarily follow that people are to invoke or pray to them.

> Although the angels in heaven pray for us (as Christ Himself

also does), and in the same way also the saints on earth and perhaps those in heaven pray for us, it does not follow from this that we ought to invoke angels and saints; pray to them; keep fasts and hold festivals for them; celebrate Masses, make sacrifices, establish churches, altars, or worship services for them; serve them in still other ways; and consider them as helpers in time of need, assign all kinds of assistance to them, and attribute a specific function to particular saints as the papists teach and do. This is idolatry. Such honour belongs to God alone.[50]

Flowing out of their worship and praise to God, the good angels are to be God's ministers in the world and in the church. Since they have been confirmed in their goodness, their will perfectly coincides with the will of God. Their sole objective is to accomplish what is good, according to God's will.[51] This results then in their faithful service toward man, which is not based upon their love for mankind, but upon their great love for God.[52]

Indeed, the perpetual bliss of the angels (as they experience the beatific vision) does not consist in idleness. They participate in willing and joyful service to God and to His people on earth. They are employed to promote the work of the church and to protect her servants (Daniel 6:22; Acts 5:18-20, 12:7-9). They are also called upon to minister to all who are faithful and walk in the way of the Lord (Psalm 34:7, 91:11), so that they may be given eternal life (Hebrews 1:14; Luke 16:22). If God were to open peoples' eyes as He did the eyes of the youth recorded in 2 Kings:16-17, they too would see the multitude of guardian angels that encamp around God's people. Once again, however, there is no Word of God which tells people that they are to call upon these angels for help directly. Nor are they to be worshiped and adored.[53]

It is important to remember that God does not have angels carry out His bidding because He is in need of their service, but because it pleases Him to have it so. Scripture particularly reveals that angels serve children (Matthew 18:10), the believers in their work and calling (Psalm 91:11-12), and the dying, who are carried to Abraham's bosom as mentioned in Luke 16:22. As to whether each person on earth, or even every Christian, has a guardian angel, there is no definitive answer, for passages such as Matthew 18:10 and Acts 12:15 are inconclusive.[54] Daphne Mould proposes that each person is assigned a guardian angel at birth. She also postulates that this guardianship takes on a new and more intimate nature after an individual is baptized. This may be reflected in the fact that the early Christian writers strongly associated angelic activity with the Sacraments. They believed the angels to be present and to rejoice whenever someone was baptized. Indeed, those undergoing instruction for baptism were urged to pray that the angels would specially guard and protect them and that the angels would pray to God on their behalf.[55]

It is this belief that God sends guardian angels to protect mankind that has been altered by New Age angelphiles. Many books and movies abound with various angel rescue stories. Deffner relates a story of which he is aware:

> Late at night a man lay in wait to kill his pastor. But he did not complete the deed. Some days later he confessed to the pastor what he had planned to do. "But why didn't you carry out your plan and kill me?" asked the pastor. "Because of the other person who was with you," replied the man. "But I was alone!" said the pastor. "No, you were not. I distinctly saw the other person."[56]

Humans should be thankful to God for their guardian angels' care. Not all purported incidents may truly be angelic appearances, though they may be unexplainable. However, it is important to remember that the protective ministry of God's angels occurs constantly, often in less dramatic ways.

> A pastor exclaimed to another pastor on greeting him, "Wow! I almost had a horrible accident on the way to the conference. My car was nearly broadsided! But God's holy angels were with me and my life was spared!"
> "That's not so unusual," said the other pastor. "Absolutely nothing happened to me on the way to the conference!"[57]

As Luther once preached, "if the beloved angels were not always there standing guard over and protecting us, we could well succumb to death ten times over in just one hour."[58] (For more examples of popular angel stories see appendix D).

At God's discretion and direction, angels protect humans in many unique ways (Daniel 6:22). "Angels protect and deliver God's people. They guard our bodies and direct us in the right path. They open our eyes to sudden danger and help us in our physical weakness. They encourage us and minister to us in times of distress and need (Acts 12:5-11, 8:26, 10:1-7)."[59] It is also taught in Scripture that angels serve and protect people from all danger and harm in both the political (Daniel 10:13; Isaiah 37:36) and domestic estates (Psalm 34:7; Matthew 18:10).[60] In fact, in the *Lutheran Worship* hymnal, there is a specific petition "For Home and Family," which asks for the protection of God's holy angels. "Visit, we implore you, O Lord, the homes in which your people dwell, and keep far from them all harm and danger. Grant us to dwell together in peace under the protection of your holy angels, and may your blessing be with us forever; through Jesus Christ, our Lord."[61]

One of the most special ministries of angels is to the Christian church. They revere and promote the message of salvation (Luke 2:13; 1 Peter 1:12; Ephesians 3:10); rejoice over repentant sinners (Luke 15:10); minister God's Word to people (Deuteronomy 33:2; Luke 2:10-12; Galatians 3:19); protect the saints of God (Jude 9); are present at public worship (1 Corinthians 11:10; 1 Timothy 5:21f); and will at last announce the final judgement (Matthew 25:31; 1 Thessalonians 4:16) and assist in its execution (Matthew 13:41-42, 50, 24:31, 25:31; Mark 13:27).[62]

Concerning the hierarchy of angels first proposed by Pseudo-Dionysius in the sixth century, there is not much to relate on the basis of Scripture. Some people continue to believe in different ranks and orders of angels (with differing functions), based upon various Scriptural passages (Isaiah 6:2-3; Hebrews 9:5; Colossians 1:16; Ephesians 1:21; 1 Thessalonians 4:16; and Jude 9).[63] An example is Leavell, who holds that God's will is carried out in different categories by different angels (Seraphim purify man; Cherubim are protectors of God's glory; the Archangel is God's tool of vengeance and judgment, and a warrior).[64] However, whether or not these truly represent separate classifications of angels is unknown, nor should it be speculated about.[65] People are unable to determine the number of the ranks or their precise difference because the Bible does not provide sufficient information. Luther and the dogmaticians held that the concept of the nine orders or choirs of angels was uncertain.[66]

There are only two different kinds of angels for certain: the good angels and the evil angels. The fallen angels also have distinct functions to perform. Evil angels harm man in his body (Luke 13:11, 16), in his earthly possessions (Job 1:12f), and in his soul (John 13:27) as the devil tries to work unbelief in man. In particular, the evil angels especially direct their fury against the church of Christ as they constantly seek to destroy it (Matthew 16:18); try to prevent humans from accepting the Word of God (Luke 8:12); spread false doctrine (Matthew 13:25); and incite persecutions against the Kingdom of Christ (Revelation 12:7). In particular, Satan has harmed the church by inflicting the tyranny and doctrinal perversions of the anti-Christ upon her (2 Thessalonians 2). In addition to this, Satan and his minions trouble the political estate (1 Chronicles 21:1) and the domestic estate (1 Timothy 4:1-3; Job 1:11-19) with the express purpose of ruining the church.[67] Luther held that all Christians should expect Satan and his angels to attack them because he fervently desires to stop the spread of the Gospel.[68]

It is of note, however, that God continues to be in control of all angelic activity, whether of good or bad angels. God uses the evil angels for His own purposes. He uses them at times to punish the godless (2 Thessalonians 2:11-12) as well as to try the believers (Job 1:7f; 2 Corinthians 12:7).[69] Luther firmly believed that God could and did use angels to punish the wicked. In his preface to the Smalcald Articles he writes, "It horrifies and frightens me that Christ might cause a council of angels to descend upon Germany and totally destroy us all, like Sodom and Gomorrah, because we mock him so blasphemously with the council."[70]

In terms of the final judgement, God's angels also have specific duties to perform. They will sound the trumpet of God (Matthew 24:31; 1 Corinthians 15:51-52) heralding the approach of Christ. They are then to gather the people from all corners of the earth (Matthew 25:31-32; Mark 13:27) to bring them before God the Judge. They shall also assist Christ in separating the good from the evil (Matthew 13:49; Luke 12:9; Jude 14-15). Finally, the angels shall cast the evildoers into hell following the judgement (Matthew 13:41-42, 49-50). Though, of course, it is Christ who judges and raises people from the dead, yet the angels are His ministering servants, assisting Him in this endeavour.[71]

Due to the fall of mankind into sin, there is much pain and suffering in this life. However, people's faith and trust are to be in God alone and not in a visible angel or a miraculous deliverance. Whether Christians ever witness an angel or not, they can be absolutely certain of God's love for them. For the Christian, life is not to be a series of outward supernatural interventions (other than Christ's continual mediation on our behalf, which we receive through the Word and the Sacraments). Even if one does experience an angel, it should not be expected to become a regular occurrence as many popular books espouse. Indeed, the more trials that Christians face and survive without outward angelic aid, the more they learn to trust God and His Word rather than experience. For their strength comes not from angels, but from Jesus Christ.[72]

The doctrine of angels should not be classified as a fundamental article of faith. People are saved by the grace of God through their faith in Christ's propitiatory sacrifice on their behalf, not their faith in the existence of angels and their services. However, as a Christian develops in his or her faith through the reading of the Holy Scriptures, the doctrine of the angels is connected to the central article of faith in Christ. It then would be inconsistent for a person to accept the doctrine of Christ and reject the doctrine of angels.[73] Still, there are many people who have many questions about angels. It is the church's responsibility to provide Scriptural answers, whenever possible, to the many questions concerning the nature and function of these spiritual beings.

> *Increase, we plead, our song of praise for angel hosts that guard our days;*
> *Teach us to ceaselessly adore, to serve as they do evermore.*[74]

Chapter Notes: Chapter 3

1. Landrum P. Leavell, *Angels, Angels, Angels* (Nashville: Broadman Press, 1973), 9.
2. Robert W. Jenson, *Systematic Theology*, vol. 2, *The Works of God* (New York: Oxford University Press, 1999), 112-113.
3. Richard C. Jahn, "The Doctrine of the Angels," in *The Abiding Word: An Anthology of Doctrinal Essays for the Years 1954-1955*, vol. 3 (St. Louis: Concordia Publishing House, 1960), 185.
4. John Theodore Mueller, *Christian Dogmatics: A Handbook of Doctrinal Theology for Pastors, Teachers, and Laymen* (St. Louis: Concordia Publishing House, 1951), 196.
5. Jahn, 186-187.
6. Andrew J. Bandstra, *In the Company of Angels: What the Bible Teaches What You Need to Know* (Grand Rapids: CRC Publications, 1995), 21.
7. Psalm 148:2, 5.
8. Jahn, 185.
9. Formula of Concord, Epitome VIII.35 in *The Book of Concord*, ed. Robert Kolb and Timothy J. Wengert (Minneapolis: Fortress Press, 2000), 513.
10. Mueller, 196-197.
11. Edward W. A. Koehler, *A Summary of Christian Doctrine: A Popular Presentation of the Teachings of the Bible* (Detroit: Louis H. Koehler, 1939; second revised printing in Oakland: Alfred W. Koehler, 1952), 44 (page citations are to the reprint edition).
12. Francis Pieper, *Christian Dogmatics*, vol. 1 (St. Louis: Concordia Publishing House, 1950), 500.
13. Mueller, 197.
14. Bandstra, 20.
15. Bandstra, 20-21.
16. Lewis Sperry Chafer, *Systematic Theology*, vol. 2 (Grand Rapids: Kregel Publications, 1993), 8.
17. Hope MacDonald, *When Angels Appear* (Grand Rapids: Daybreak Books, 1982), 17-18.
18. Mueller, 197.
19. Mueller, 198.
20. Jahn, 190.

21. Leavell, 22.
22. Daphne D.C. Pochin Mould, *Angels of God: Their Rightful Place in the Modern World* (New York: The Devin-Adair Company, 1963), 16.
23. Pieper, 504.
24. Mueller, 44.
25. Mueller, 201.
26. Mueller, 198.
27. Jahn, 190.
28. Martin Chemnitz, *Loci Theologici*, vol. 1, trans. J.A.O. Preus (St. Louis: Concordia Publishing House, 1989), 178.
29. Pieper, 501.
30. The beatific vision is "The supernatural act of the created intellect by which the beatified angels and souls are united to God in a direct, intuitive, and clear knowledge of the Triune God as He is in Himself." M.J. Redle, "Beatific Vision," in *New Catholic Encyclopedia*, vol. 2 (Washington, D.C.: The Catholic University of America, 1976), 186.
31. Mueller, 197.
32. Pieper, 502.
33. Mueller, 198.
34. Smalcald Articles, Second Part II.15 in Kolb and Wengert (Minneapolis: Fortress Press, 2000), 304.
35. Chemnitz, 174.
36. Mueller 198-201.
37. Mueller, 200.
38. Koehler, 46.
39. Koehler, 46.
40. Koehler, 46-47.
41. Mueller, 196.
42. Donald L. Deffner, *The Truth About Angels* (Kitchener, ON: The International Lutheran Laymen's League, 1996), 15-17.
43. MacDonald, 17, 19.
44. Jahn, 190.
45. Chafer, 21.
46. Formula of Concord, Solid Declaration VI.6 in Kolb and Wengert, 588.
47. MacDonald, 23-24.
48. Mueller, 202.
49. Michael Rogness, "A Fascination with Angels," *Word & World* 18, no. 1 (1998): 60.
50. Smalcald Articles, Second Part II.26-27 in Kolb and Wengert (Minneapolis: Fortress Press, 2000), 305-306.
51. Pieper, 506.
52. Leavell, 39.
53. Koehler, 45-46.
54. Pieper, 506-507.
55. Mould, 17-18.
56. Deffner, 18-19.
57. Deffner, 19.
58. Martin Luther, "The Day of St. Michael and All Angels: Second Sermon, 1534," in *Sermons of*

Martin Luther: The House Postils, ed. Eugene F.A. Klug, trans. Eugene F.A. Klug, et al, vol 3, *Sermons on Gospel Texts for the Fifteenth through Twenty-Sixth Sundays after Trinity, the Festival of Christ's Nativity, and Other Occasions* (Grand Rapids: Baker Books, 1996), 389

59. MacDonald, 22.
60. Mueller, 201.
61. "For Home and Family" in *Lutheran Worship*, prepared by the Commission on Worship of the Lutheran Church—Missouri Synod (St. Louis: Concordia Publishing House, 1982), 129.
62. Mueller, 201-202.
63. Jahn, 192.
64. Leavell, 70-72.
65. Jahn, 192.
66. Pieper, 504.
67. Mueller, 202-203.
68. Large Catechism, Third Part III.65 in Kolb and Wengert (Minneapolis: Fortress Press, 2000), 448-449.
69. Pieper, 510.
70. Smalcald Articles, Preface.11 in Kolb and Wengert, 299.
71. Jahn, 239-241.
72. MacDonald, 27-28, 30-31.
73. Pieper, 498.
74. Phillip Melanchthon, "Lord God, to You We All Give Praise," trans. Emanuel Cronenwett in *Lutheran Worship*, #189.

Conclusion

> For He will command His angels concerning you to
> guard you in all your ways;
> they will lift you up in their hands, so that
> you will not strike your foot against a stone.
> (Psalm 91:11-12)

Having discussed the historical understanding of angels, current NewAge thinking concerning angels, and Biblical teaching, it has been shown how vastly different New Age spirituality and Christian theology are regarding angelology. As Duane Garrett writes, "Angels are real. Some people have seen them. They continue to influence human life. They can and do protect people. If this is so, why should anyone have concerns about the new interest in angels?"[1]

The Bible describes angels in functional terms. It describes many things that angels do, but says very little about their origins. Throughout Scripture, the emphasis is placed upon the sovereignty of God the Creator over all of His creation, including the angel hosts of heaven. The Bible exhorts people to recognize and remember that only Christ is the Saviour of the world, that He alone is the perfect mediator, and that only He, and never the angels, can fully identify with humanity (as He is both true God and true Man).[2]

Angels have been prominent in people's thoughts for centuries, from the early church until the present time. People are fascinated with angels. Due to this intense focus upon angels, and the Bible's limited revelation concerning their origin and function, people have freely invented stories about angels in order to fill in the gaps. Presently, people are supposedly contacting angels to gain new revelation into the hidden workings of the universe, and using angels as guides to the Supreme Source. Indeed, in the western postmodern world there is a resurgence of New Age spirituality.[3]

This New Age spirituality concerning angels is contrary to what the holy Scriptures teach. According to the Bible people are to have nothing to do with spirits or even claim to know them (Leviticus 19:31). Nor are people to seek after the secret knowledge of the things that God has chosen not to reveal to His people (Deuteronomy 29:29; 1 Corinthians 4:6; 1 Timothy 4:7). Humanity is "to avoid seeking contact with spirits altogether. It is not just that we might be deceived or that the angel might turn out to be a devil. All fascination with angels and every desire to get to know them is a distraction from Christ."[4] As Karl Barth states:

> Angels cannot, then, speak words which as their own are the words of God. They cannot do works which as their own are divine works. They cannot save, redeem or liberate the earthly creature. They cannot forgive even the smallest sin, or remove even the slightest pain. They can do nothing to bring about the reconciliation of the world with God. Nor are they judges of the world. They did not create it. They can neither be wrathful nor gracious toward it. They did not establish the covenant between God and man, and they cannot fulfill, maintain, renew, or confirm it. They do not overcome death. They do not rule the history of salvation, or universal history, or any history….They are heavenly creatures, but they are creatures no less strictly than all earthly creatures. If they speak the Word of God and do the work of God, it is never as their own. If they have power to do so (as they have); if they themselves are heavenly powers, it is as representatives, in the revelation and exercise of the one power of God Himself.

They never take the central position, but always leave it open for the One who alone can occupy it.[5]

Those who desire to make contact with angels and become their "friends" deny the sovereignty and all-sufficiency of God. An angel who takes on the role of one's instructor, guide, or saviour is not really functioning as an angel at all. Humanity has only one God and Saviour. The very idea that an angel can be one's close companion and guide and yet not become one's god is a delusion. Regardless what one may claim, the spiritual being that a person loves, from whom one learns, and who gives a person spiritual protection, is surely one's god, whether or not he or she calls him that. God has revealed to the world His name and His Son, who is the way of redemption, holiness, and true spirituality. Jesus Christ alone is the way, the truth, and the life.[6] (John 14:6).

So then, where do angels fit into Christian theology? Why even bother to believe that angels exist, if there is so much uncertainty in the Bible concerning them? What is the benefit to the Christian? The fact is that angels are God's creatures, just as people are. However, He has given them a specific purpose in relation to human beings, their fellow creatures. Angels protect and deliver God's people from harm and danger. They are ministers of His grace in times of distress and need.[7] They are servants of His Gospel, but they are not the Gospel in and of themselves. Christians should "rejoice and take comfort in their service and carefully avoid grieving them (1 Corinthians 11:10; 1 Timothy 5:21)."[8] Indeed, even the evil angels serve the purpose of the propagation of the holy Gospel. As Francis Pieper states, "Finally, we should bear in mind that all that the Bible says of the evil angels and their eternal punishment serves the ends of divine compassion. Its purpose is to impress on men the necessity of repentance and of faith in Him who by His blood ransomed mankind not for hell, but for heaven."[9]

The stress which the postmodern world places upon experience as the guide to personal truth makes it challenging for Christians to dialogue with postmodernists.[10] Christians are not to hold personal experience, but Scripture as the source of all truth. Therefore, angelic encounters are not to be the firm foundation of a person's faith. Whether or not one has an angelic visitation is irrelevant in terms of God's great love for humanity. His love has been made certain through Jesus Christ, not through His angels. People's response of love, therefore, should also not be affected by angelic encounters. As Hope MacDonald writes, "Will we love and trust God more if we see an angel tonight? No. We love Him even if we never see an angel. God wants us to love Him for who He is [and what He has done for us in Christ], not because we have received signs and wonders [through angels]."[11]

Though the increase of New Age spirituality in the west should be treated by the church with some concern, it should also be viewed as an incredible opportunity. Postmodernists are on a spiritual quest. It is the church's opportunity and duty to fulfill this spiritual hunger. People are dabbling "in the new spirituality because they want real spirituality. They do not want only to *hear* about holiness and transcendence and power beyond themselves; they want to *experience* these things."[12] The question before the church, then, is how to engage people in the culture. Gene Edward Veith, Jr. believes that confessionalism is the answer—a living and vibrant confessionalism that states what it believes and readily includes the experiential. He states, "Confessionalism should not mean 'dead orthodoxy,' the insistence on some kind of doctrinal purity at the expense of a warm, personal faith. The goal should be 'live orthodoxy,' a faith that is both experiential and grounded in truth, with room for both feelings and the intellect."[13]

In terms of angelology, this is important. Though Christians do not miss out on the many gifts that God has to offer if they do not encounter an angel, angels are important. Certainly, belief in the existence of angels is not a fundamental article of faith, yet "when a man [or woman] has become a Christian and reads the Bible, he [or she] will find in it, from Genesis to Revelation, the doctrine of angels, side by side with the central article of Christ, the Saviour of sinners."[14] Angels were created to serve God and to benefit mankind. They are a part of the glory of heaven that Christians see by faith. By believing in the reality of these spiritual servants of God, Christians are led to understand that there is another glory which surpasses anything in this world. Though God does not need angels, the universe is far richer because of them. The angels add to the glory of the universe in the same way that trees, mountains, and even humans do. Above all, it is imperative for Christians to remember that angels are our guardians and servants, sent by God. They are another of God's tools to provide Christians with comfort and peace in time of need.[15]

Christians have been blessed by God through the ministry of His holy angels. Christians are assured of God's protection through the ministration of these spiritual beings. Though Christians should never worship angels (and there is a profound difference between believing *in* angels, which is idolatry, and holding proper beliefs *concerning* angelic beings, which is appropriate), and though angels do not even desire people's worship or prayers, Christians can and should freely pray to God to send them divine aid through His angels. Indeed, they are a special part of God's plan to give His people comfort, peace, and hope—to which His faithful children joyfully respond to Him with utmost thanks and praise.

I give thanks to you, my heavenly Father, through Jesus Christ your dear Son, that you have graciously protected me today, and I ask you to forgive me all my sins, where I have done wrong, and graciously protect me tonight. For into your hands I commend myself: my body, my soul, and all that is mine. Let your holy angel be with me, so that the wicked foe may have no power over me. Amen.[16]

Chapter Notes: Conclusion

1. Duane A. Garrett, *Angels and the New Spirituality* (Nashville: Broadman & Holman Publishers, 1995), 234.
2. Garrett, 234.
3. Garrett, 235.
4. Garrett, 235.
5. Karl Barth, *Church Dogmatics*, vol. 3, *The Doctrine of Creation*, ed. G.W. Bromiley and T.F. Torrance, trans. G.W. Bromiley and R.J. Ehrlich, part 3 (Edinburgh: T & T Clark Ltd., 1983), 460.
6. Garrett, 236.
7. Hope MacDonald, *When Angels Appear* (Grand Rapids: Daybreak Books, 1982), 22.
8. Francis Pieper, *Christian Dogmatics*, vol. 1 (St. Louis: Concordia Publishing House, 1950), 507.
9. Pieper, 511.
10. Matt Ziprick, "The Gospel for a Postmodern Culture" (M. Div. Thesis, Concordia Lutheran Seminary, Edmonton, AB, 2002), 3.
11. MacDonald, 32.
12. Garrett, 237.
13. Gene Edward Veith, Jr., *Postmodern Times: A Christian Guide to Contemporary Thought and Culture* in *Turning Point Christian Worldview Series*, ed. Marvin Olasky (Wheaton: Crossway Books, 1994), 220.
14. Pieper, 498.
15. Garrett, 239-240.
16. Small Catechism, VI.5, in *The Book of Concord*, ed. Robert Kolb and Timothy J. Wengert (Minneapolis: Fortress Press, 2000), 364.

APPENDIX A

HIERARCHY OF ANGELS

Angelic Orders and Hierarchy[1]

A few examples of the arrangement of the angelic orders proposed by various Latin writers, along with Dionysius the Areopagite, are given below. The Seraphim is always the highest order or the order closest to God, while the Angels are usually the lowest. Note that, significantly, the orders are not always listed from lowest to highest.

Ambrose	Jerome	Gregory the Great	Dionysius the Areopagite
Angels	Archangels	Angels	Seraphim
Archangels	Angels	Archangels	Cherubim
Dominions	Thrones	Thrones	Thrones
Powers	Dominions	Dominions	Dominions
	Powers	Virtues	Powers
	Cherubim	Principalities	Authorities
	Seraphim	Powers	Principalities
		Cherubim	Archangels
		Seraphim	Angels

[1] *Angelic Spirituality: Medieval Perspectives on the Ways of Angels*, introduced and trans. by Steven Chase in the *The Classics of Western Spirituality*, ed. Bernard McGinn (New York: Paulist Press, 2002), 18-19.

APPENDIX B

RITUALS OF INVOCATION

Paul Roland's Exercise[1]

Exercise: The Angel of Forgiveness

Begin as usual with the basic relaxation, grounding and clearing exercise from Chapter 2.

When you feel sufficiently relaxed visualize yourself standing on a mountain top where the air is clear, fresh and invigorating. Far below, the clouds obscure the earth from view. On a ledge just below you mountain goats graze on exotic-coloured flowers which grow through the cracks in the stone. The tinkling of the bells around the necks of the goats is the only sound you can hear in the stillness.

You turn away from the edge and walk across the plateau to where a small wooden bridge straddles a sparkling stream. You begin to cross, pausing half-way to enjoy the sound of the running water which lulls you into an even deeper state of relaxation. Finally you step onto the other side where stands a small temple to which you feel irresistibly drawn. You climb ten steps and enter the temple where the feeling of serenity and well-being is almost overwhelming. The scent of incense and flowers is intoxicating. Everywhere candles are burning with not a breath of wind to unsteady their flame. All is stillness and serenity.

To each side sit a line of people just like you in quiet contemplation. They bow their heads with respect in acknowledgement of your presence as you enter and walk towards the altar which lies at the far end of the temple. Before the altar are baskets of fruit and flowers and pictures of angels who have served and guided all those who have come to the temple this day. Perhaps you respond to one of these celestial beings?

You bow before an awesome statue of an archangel which rises behind the

---

[1] Paul Roland, *Angels: A Piatkus Guide* (London: Judy Piatkus Publishers, Ltd., 1999), 75-77.

altar, but this is not idol worship, you are acknowledging the Divine potential in yourself which it symbolizes. On the floor in front of you is a cushion with sheaves of paper and a pen. Kneel down and open your heart centre in the sacred space, allowing whatever troubles you to rise up and find expression in words or perhaps even in a symbol of some sort. Feel it being plucked like a stone from the emotional centre of your being as you write down your thoughts, your plea for forgiveness, or your question. Now, what do you replace the empty space with? What do you take from this place of peace and forgiveness?

See yourself folding the paper into a taper and placing it in the flame of a candle which lies by the feet of the angel statue. Watch the paper blacken and see the smoke rise into the shaft of light which breaks through the window above the angel's head. Drop the ash into a bowl of water and know that you are relieved of guilt or of whatever has been needlessly troubling you. Accept that any mistakes you made were an essential part of your learning in life and forgive yourself. Know too that in asking you are forgiven and relieved of this burden now and for ever. If you asked a question know with certainty that the answer will come, perhaps during your dreams this night.

Now gradually become aware of your surroundings once again, sense your body sitting in the chair and focus your breathing. Count down slowly from ten to one and when you are ready, open your eyes.

John Price's Meditation[2]

Meditation for the Angel of Materiality and Temptation

As I call forth the Angel of Materiality and Temptation, I see his light ahead, and I move toward it with confidence. And now before me stands this Emissary of Cosmic Law. In my own words and in my own way I express my gratitude for his guidance and protection, for helping me to be in this world, though not of it, and to be one with the thought divine.

I now listen to the words of the angel. I hear. I understand.

I embrace the angel in appreciation and then move deeper in consciousness

---

[2]John Randolph Price, *The Angels Within Us: A Spiritual Guide to the Twenty-Two Angels that Govern Our Lives* (New York: Fawcett Columbine, 1993), 217-218.

to meet my Master Self. And in this Presence I ponder these thoughts:

I am the instrument through which the Master I AM expresses, and I place my dependence on this Holy One within rather than on anything in the outer world. I understand that the only responsibility that I have in life is to be conscious of my God-Self and that that Self will then meet all of my responsibilities through me. I realize that as long as there is a human sense of being, I must not rely on that sense to free me from lack and limitation. My reliance must be totally on the Christ within, who is eternally radiating the Energy of All Good into my world.

I now live as an open channel for You, my Lord and Master Self, without spiritual pride, without relying on unrealized truth to change my world, without distortions of reality. I will live in oneness with You as I walk the earth, enjoying every moment of my journey and knowing that the Awakening will soon take place. And I will emerge as the one who says, "He who sees me sees the Father."

I now listen to the words of my Holy Self. (Listen in the silence.)

Albert Haldane's and Simha Seraya's Invocation[3]
Invocation of the Angel OVA-MA-EL (August 12 – 16)

O Angel Ova-Ma-El, confer upon me the lucidity to converse with the trees, the planets, the suns, and the angels.
Angel Ova-Ma-El, guide me, elevate my soul, dissolve my oblivion and fears, encourage my impulses toward the source of divine streams.
O Angel Ova-Ma-El, thank you, for the riches you provide, the thoughts that dwell in my soul, and these words chanting your glory.

---

[3] Albert Haldane and Simha Seraya with Barbara Lagowski, *Angel Signs: A Celestial Guide to the Powers of Your Own Guardian Angel* (New York: HarperSanFrancisco, 2002), 103.

APPENDIX C

RITUAL OF EVOCATION

The Evocation of Hagiel[1]

Before attempting this ritual you should have familiarized yourself with it so well that you can visualize everything with your eyes shut. Make a checklist of all the necessary items and have them ready. Purify yourself in advance, as outlined on pages 108-109. The ritual is to be performed on a Friday night at 10 o'clock, the day and hour of Venus.
Put a green light bulb in the light of the room you will use and sprinkle saltwater around the edges of the room. After bathing, put on a green robe and a copper necklace with a green stone. Anoint your wrists, breast, and temples with apricot oil mixed with a drop each of sandalwood and cinnamon oils.
On the east side of the circle you will make, place a triangle of green silk with equal sides about 18 inches (47 cm) long. On the cloth place a seven-pointed star cut from green card. Make a circle around the cloth (clockwise) with 49 green-coloured stones (you can substitute small flour balls made with water, white flour, and green vegetable dye). Forty-nine is Hagiel's number (seven) squared.
Place a green candle at the east, south, west, and north points of this circle. Light them and extinguish all other lights except the green light. Burn some cinnamon and sandalwood. Now face the east, with the cloth a few feet in front of you, and perform the Kabbalistic Cross as explained on pages 110-111. Then perform Ritual of the Pentagram as explained on pages 111-113, at the end of which you should find yourself facing east. Now you may invoke the lovely Angel Hagiel. The invocation is simple: Intone her name silently seven times in your mind (ha-gee-el); then whisper her name seven times; then call her name seven times in ringing tones, concluding, equally loud, "Come thou before me!" If you have been in calm, confident command of the whole process up until this point, you should observe a beautiful female form materialize before your eyes.
You will likely be stunned by her presence, but her manner is always sweet and affectionate. Keep control of yourself—remember you are in charge!—

---

[1] Francis Melville, *The Book of Angels* (Hauppage: Barron's Educational Series Inc., 2001), 122-123.

and ask her to bestow the gift of unconditional love on the person of your choice. You may now thank her and bid her farewell. She will slowly fade from sight.

If she failed to appear, try again! Remember, it is what you bring, in terms of powerful, confident, contained energy that determines your success in evoking angels.

APPENDIX D

ANGEL STORIES

Donald Deffner's Angel Story[1]

A child fell in a deep well. She could not swim. Later, family members searching for her found her on the grass beside the well, soaking wet. The girl described the person who pulled her out as "all shiny and white."

Cindy Knecht's Angel Story[2]

There isn't a day that goes by that I don't see, hear, or smell an angel. One day, I was sitting in my room trying to get in touch with my angel friends when I saw a lightning bolt. I ran from the room and cried. "Something is going to happen to one of us," I told my niece, "and it's not going to be good."

At the time, I was having problems with my foot. I thought I had sprained it and decided to ignore the pain and go about my business. For the next few day, it smelled like a funeral parlor in my house. I told my niece, "I smell a dead person. One of us is going to die."

The pain in my foot was so severe by that time that I had to see a doctor. That's when I learned that I had cancer of the foot and leg. It was so intertwined in my muscles and nerves that they had to amputate.

I believe it was the bolt from the blue that made me sit up and take notice. The angels warned me that day, in a loud and startling way. Thank God for the scare. If I'd waited, the cancer would have killed me. So when I told my niece, "someone is going to die," I meant it was ME.

Now I see the doctor regularly. I don't test the angels or try to contact them. They'll find me when I need them. Amen.

---

[1] Donald L. Deffner, *The Truth About Angels* (Kitchener, ON: The International Lutheran Laymen's League, 1996), 19.

[2] Cindy Knecht's personal story in *Angel Talk* (Boca Raton, FL: American Media Mini Mags, 2000), 35-36.

An Angel Story Collected by Hope MacDonald[3]

During World War II, George was a navigator on a B-24 bomber called The Liberator and was stationed in Italy. On one particular mission, his plane was flying over central Europe. As they approached the target area to be bombed, he felt a strong hand on his shoulder and heard a voice say to him, "Get up and go to the back of the plane."

In the brief moments that he was back there, a limited antiaircraft firing took place over the target area. When George returned to the front of the plane, he noticed a shell three inches in diameter had blown a hole in the ceiling of the plane and right through the navigator's seat.

To this day, he is confident God sent an angel to tell him to go to the back of the plane at that specific moment. He has remained conscious of God's hand on his life through the years and it has greatly added to his faith and trust in Him.

---

[3] Hope MacDonald, *When Angels Appear* (Grand Rapids: Daybreak Books, 1982), 53.

BIBLIOGRAPHY

Bandstra, Andrew J. *In the Company of Angels: What the Bible Teaches What You Need to Know.* Grand Rapids: CRC Publications, 1995.

Barth, Karl. *Church Dogmatics.* Vol. 3, *The Doctrine of Creation.* Edited by G.W. Bromiley and T.F. Torrance. Translated by G.W. Bromiley and R.J. Ehrlich. Part 3. Edinburgh: T & T Clark Ltd., 1983.

Brown, Francis. s.v. "מַלְאָךְ" *The New Brown—Driver—Briggs—Gesenius Hebrew and English Lexicon with an Appendix Containing the Biblical Aramaic.* N.P.: Christian Copyrights, Inc., 1983.

Burnham, Sophy. *A Book of Angels: Reflections on Angels Past and Present and True Stories of How They Touch Our Lives.* New York: Ballantine Books, 1990.

Chafer, Lewis Sperry. *Systematic Theology.* Vol. 2. Grand Rapids: Kregel Publications, 1993.

Chemnitz, Martin. *Loci Theologici.* Translated by J.A.O. Preus. Vol. 1. St. Louis: Concordia Publishing House, 1989.

Cousins, Ewert H. Preface to *Angelic Spirituality: Medieval Perspectives on the Ways of Angels.* Introduced and translated by Steven Chase. The Classics of Western Spirituality, ed. Bernard McGinn. New York: Paulist Press, 2002.

Crombie, F., trans. "The Pastor of Hermas: Visions," 3.4.1. *The Ante-Nicene Fathers: Translations from the Writings of the Fathers down to A.D. 325.* Edited by Alexander Roberts and James Donaldson. Vol. 2, *Fathers of the Second Century: Hermas, Tatian, Athenagoras, Theophilus, and Clement of Alexandria (Entire).* Grand Rapids: Wm. B. Eerdmans Publishing Company, 1979.

Deffner, Donald L. *The Truth About Angels.* Kitchener: The International Lutheran Laymen's League, 1996.

Easton, Karyn. "Angel Magic." WWW Page, http://www.paranormality.com/angel_magic.shtml [3 March 2003].

Fisher, George Park. *History of Christian Doctrine*. New York: Charles Scribner's Sons, 1896.

"For Home and Family." *Lutheran Worship*. Prepared by the Commission on Worship of the Lutheran Church—Missouri Synod. St. Louis: Concordia Publishing House, 1982.

Freedman, D.N. and B.E. Willoughby. s.v. "מַלְאָךְ," *Theological Dictionary of the Old Testament*. Vol. 8. Edited by G. Johannes Botterweck, Helmer Ringgren, and Heinz-Josep Fabry. Translated by Douglas W. Stott. Grand Rapids: Wm. B. Eerdmans Publishing Co., 1997.

Freeman, Eileen Elias. *Angelic Healing: Working with Your Angels to Heal Your Life*. New York: Warner Books, 1994.

Friberg, Timothy, Barbara Friberg, and Neva F. Miller, ed. *Analytical Lexicon of the Greek New Testament*. s.v. "ἄγγελος" Grand Rapids: Baker Books, 2000.

Garrett, Duane A. *Angels and the New Spirituality*. Nashville: Broadman & Holman Publishers, 1995.

Garrigou-Lagrange, Reginald. *The Trinity and God the Creator: A Commentary on St. Thomas' Theological Summa, Ia, q. 27-119*. Tranlated by Frederic C. Eckhoff. London: B. Herder Book Co., 1952.

Gonzalez, Justo L. *A History of Christian Thought*. Vol. 2, *From Augustine to the Eve of the Reformation*, rev. ed. Nashville: Abingdon Press, 1971.

_____. *A History of Christian Thought*. Vol. 3, *From the Protestant Reformation to the Twentieth Century*, rev. ed. Nashville: Abingdon Press, 1975.

Google Search. "Angel Magic." WWW Page, http://www.google.ca/search"=%22angel+magic%22&ie=UTF-8&oe=UTF-8&hl=... [3 March 2003].

_____. "Angelology." WWW Page, http://www.google.ca/search?hl=en&ie=UTF-8&oe=UTF-8&q=angelology&meta= [3 March 2003].

_____. "Angels." WWW Page, http://www.google.ca/search?q=angels&ie=UTF-8&oe=UTF-8&hl=en&meta= [3 March 2003].

Grundmann, Walter. s.v. "ἄγγελος in the Greek and Hellenistic World." *Theological Dictionary of the New Testament*. Vol. 1. Edited by Gerhard Kittel and Geoffrey W. Bromiley. Translated by Geoffrey W. Bromiley. Grand Rapids: Wm. B. Eerdmans Publishing Co., 1964.

Hagenbach, K.R. *History of Doctrines*. Translated by Henry B. Smith. Vol. 1. New York: Sheldon and Company, 1861.

Haldane, Albert, Simha Serya, and Barbara Lagowski. *Angel Signs: A Celestial Guide to the Powers of Your Own Guardian Angel*. New York: HarperSanFrancisco, 2002.

Hebblethwaite, Brian. *The Christian Hope*. Grand Rapids: William B. Eerdmans Publishing Company, 1984.

Jahn, Richard C. "The Doctrine of the Angels." *The Abiding Word: An Anthology of Doctrinal Essays for the Years* 1954-1955. Vol. 3. St. Louis: Concordia Publishing House, 1960.

Jenson, Robert W. *Systematic Theology*. Vol. 2, The Works of God. New York: Oxford University Press, 1999.

Kimba. "Angelic Divination Readings." WWW Page, http://kimbasangels.com/angelreadings.html [3 March 2003].

Kittel, Gerhard. s.v. "ἄγγελος in the NT." *Theological Dictionary of the New Testament*. Vol. 1. Edited by Gerhard Kittel and Geoffrey W. Bromiley. Translated by Geoffrey W. Bromiley. Grand Rapids: Wm. B. Eerdmans Publishing Co., 1964.

Knecht, Cindy. "Personal story," in *Angel Talk*. Boca Raton: American Media Mini Mags, Inc., 2000.

Kolb, Robert and Timothy J. Wengert, ed. *The Book of Concord*. Translated by Charles Arand, et al. Minneapolis: Fortress Press, 2000.

Koehler, Edward W.A. *A Summary of Christian Doctrine: A Popular Presentation of the Teachings of the Bible*. Detroit: Louis H. Koehler, 1939. Second revised printing, Oakland: Alfred W. Koehler, 1952 (page references are to the reprint edition).

Kostlin, Julius. *The Theology of Luther in its Historical Development and Inner Harmony*. Translated by Charles E. Hay. Vol. 2. Philadelphia: Luther Publication Society, 1897. Reprint, Concordia Heritage Series, St. Louis: Concordia Publishing House, 1986 (page refer ences are to the reprint edition).

Leavell, Landrum P. *Angels, Angels, Angels*. Nashville: Broadman Press, 1973.

Luther, Martin. "The Day of St. Michael and All Angels: First Sermon, 1532." *Sermons of Martin Luther: The House Postils*. Edited by Eugene F. A. Klug. Translated by Eugene F.A. Klug, et al. Vol. 3, *Sermons on Gospel Texts for the Fifteenth through Twenty-Sixth Sundays after Trinity, the Festival of Christ's Nativity, and Other Occasions*. Grand Rapids: Baker Books, 1996.

———. "The Day of St. Michael and All Angels: Second Sermon, 1534." *Sermons of Martin Luther: The House Postils*. Edited by Eugene F. A. Klug. Translated by Eugene F.A. Klug, et al. Vol. 3, *Sermons on Gospel Texts for the Fifteenth through Twenty-Sixth Sundays after Trinity, the Festival of Christ's Nativity, and Other Occasions*. Grand Rapids: Baker Books, 1996.

———. "Lectures on Zechariah: The Latin Text" (1526). Translatd by Richard J. Dinda. *Luther's Works*. Edited by Hilton C. Oswald. Vol. 20, *Lectures on the Minor Prophets III: Zechariah*. St. Louis: Concordia Publishing House, 1973.

———. "A Mighty Fortress Is Our God." Translated by Lutheran Book of Worship. *Lutheran Worship*. Prepared by the Commission on Worship of the Lutheran Church—Missouri Synod. St. Louis: Concordia Publishing House, 1982.

MacDonald, Hope. *When Angels Appear*. Grand Rapids: Daybreak Books, 1982.

McGinn, Bernard, ed. *Angelic Spirituality: Medieval Perspectives on the Ways of Angels*. Introduced and translated by Steven Chase. The Classics of Western Spirituality. New York: Paulist Press, 2002.

McLean, Adam, ed. *A Treatise on Angel Magic: Being a Complete Transcription of Ms. Harley 6482 in the British Library*. Magnum Opus Hermetic Sourceworks #15. Grand Rapids: Phanes Press, 1990.

Melanchthon, Phillip. "Lord God, to You We All Give Praise." Translated by Emanuel Cronenwett. *Lutheran Worship*. Prepared by the Commission on Worship of the Lutheran Church—Missouri Synod. St. Louis: Concordia Publishing House, 1982.

Melville, Francis. *The Book of Angels*. Hauppage: Barron's Educational Series Inc., 2001.

Mould, Daphne D.C. Pochin. *Angels of God: Their Rightful Place in the Modern World*. New York: The Devin-Adair Company, 1963.

Mueller, John Theodore. *Christian Dogmatics: A Handbook of Doctrinal Theology for Pastors, Teachers, and Laymen*. St. Louis: Concordia Publishing House, 1951.

Noll, Stephen F. *Angels of Light, Powers of Darkness: Thinking Biblically About Angels, Satan, & Principalities*. Downers Grove, IL: InterVarsity Press, 1998.

_____. s.v. "מַלְאָךְ," New *International Dictionary of Old Testament Theology and Exegesis*. Vol. 2. Edited by Willem A. van Gemeren. Grand Rapids: Zondervan Publishing House, 1997.

Pieper, Francis. *Christian Dogmatics*. Vol. 1. St. Louis: Concordia Publishing House, 1950.

Pelikan, Jaroslav. *The Christian Tradition: A History of the Development of Doctrine*. Vol. 1, *The Emergence of the Catholic Tradition (100-600)*. Chicago: University of Chicago Press, 1971.

_____. *The Christian Tradition: A History of the Development of Doctrine*. Vol. 3, *The Growth of Medieval Theology (600-1300)*. Chicago: Chicago University Press, 1978.

_____. *The Christian Tradition: A History of the Development of Doctrine*. Vol. 4, *Reformation of Church and Dogma (1300-1700)*. Chicago: The University of Chicago Press, 1984.

Price, John Randolph. *The Angels Within Us: A Spiritual Guide to the Twenty-Two Angels that Govern Our Lives*. New York: Fawcett Columbine, 1993.

Redle, M.J. "Beatific Vision." *New Catholic Encyclopedia*. Vol. 2. Washington, D.C.: The Catholic University of America, 1967.

Roberts, Alexander, trans. "Irenaeus Against Heresies," 2.2.1. *The Ante-Nicene Fathers: Translations from the Writings of the Fathers down to A.D. 325*. Edited by Alexander Roberts and James Donaldson. Vol. 1, *The Apostolic Fathers—Justin Martyr—Irenaeus*. Grand Rapids: Wm. B. Eerdmans Publishing Company, 1981.

Rogness, Michael. "A Fascination with Angels." *Word & World* 18, no. 1 (1998): 57-61.

Roland, Paul. *Angels: A Piatkus Guide*. London: Judy Piatkus Publishers, Ltd., 1999.

Schleiermacher, Friedrich. *The Christian Faith*. Edited by H.R. Mackintosh and J.S. Stewart. Edinburgh: T & T Clart, Ltd., 1999.

Schneweis, Emil. *Angels and Demons According to Lactanius*. Washington, D.C.: The Catholic University of America Press, Inc., 1944.

Sweet, Leonard. *Postmodern Pilgrims*. Nashville: Broadman & Holman Publishers, 2000.

_____. *Soul Tsunami*. Grand Rapids: Zondervan, 1999.

Tersteegen, Gerhard. "God Himself is Present." *Lutheran Worship*. Prepared by the Commission on Worship of the Lutheran Church—Missouri Synod. St. Louis: Concordia Publishing House, 1982.

Veith, Jr., Gene Edward. *Postmodern Times: A Christian Guide to Contemporary Thought and Culture*. Turning Point Christian Worldview Series. Edited by Marvin Olasky. Wheaton: Crossway Books, 1994.

Westermann, Claus. *God's Angels Need No Wings*. Translated by David L. Scheidt. Philadelphia: Fortress Press, 1979.

Whyte, Alexander. "The Nature of Angels (I): December 18, 1870; St. George's, Edinburgh." *The Nature of Angels: Eight Addresses by Alexander Whyte*. Grand Rapids: Baker Book House, 1930; reprint ed 1976.

Ziprick, Matt. "The Gospel for a Postmodern Culture." M. Div. Thesis, Concordia Lutheran Seminary, Edmonton, 2002.

Index

Angelic, 2-3, 7-12, 14, 16-17, 21-22, 28-30, 32-36, 39, 45-46, 48, 55-56, 59

Angel Magic, 17-18, 26, 33, 35

Angelology, 2,8, 10-12, 16-20, 25-27, 29, 35, 53, 56

Angelphile(s), 32-33, 46

Apocalypticism, 9

Aquinas, Thomas, 11

Archangel(s), 12, 21, 47, 59, 61

Arian, 8, 10

Arius, 8

Astrology, 1, 39

Atheism, 8

Athenagoras, 7-9

Augustine, 8-10

Authorities, 12, 21, 59

Baptism, 46

Beatific Vision, 42-43, 45, 50

Bernard of Clairvaux, 12

Bible, 2, 7, 14, 19-20, 27, 29, 40, 42, 44, 47, 54-56

Biblical, 2-3, 7, 10, 12, 17, 19-20, 27-29, 36, 40-41, 44, 53

Bonaventure, 11

Buddhism, 28

Calvin, John, 13, 16

Celestial, 8, 12, 15, 18, 61

Chakra(s), 34

Chemnitz, Martin, 13 17

Cherubim, 12, 14, 20-21, 47, 59

Christian(s), 2, 5, 7-8, 10, 12-16, 18-19, 27-29, 31, 33, 35-36, 40, 44-45, 47-48, 53, 55-56

Church, 1, 3, 5, 7-13, 16-17, 19-20, 36, 40, 43, 45, 47-48, 54, 56

Council of Laodicea, 10

Council of Lyons, 11

Council of Nicea, 8, 10

Creator, 7, 15, 19, 40, 42, 54

Creature(s), 7, 11, 14, 16, 35, 40-42, 54-55

Cyril of Jerusalem, 9

Demi-gods, 40

Demon(s), 13, 15-17, 19-20, 31

Demonic, 3, 31

Demonism, 39

Devil(s), 9, 13-16, 19, 30, 33, 36, 42, 47, 54

Didymus of Alexandria, 9

Dionysius the Areopagite (Pseudo-Dionysius), 9, 12, 14, 16, 47, 59

Divine, 2-3, 10, 12, 15, 17, 28-32, 36, 42, 44, 54-56, 62-63

Diviner, 34

Divinity, 30

Dominions, 12, 21, 59

Enlightenment, 17-19

Epiphanius, 8

Esoteric, 1, 17, 29

Eusebius, 8

Evocation(s), 33-35, 65

Faith, 1, 8, 11-14, 40, 43, 48, 55-56, 68

Faithful, 43, 45, 56

Fortune-telling, 1, 39

Fourth Lateran Council, 11

Ghost(s), 30

Gnostic, 8, 20

God, 1-3, 5, 7-16, 18-20, 26-28, 32-33, 35-36, 39-48, 54-56, 59, 63, 67-68

Gods, 27-28, 35, 40

Goddesses, 27, 33

Gospel, 16, 48, 55

Grace, 11, 43, 48, 55

Greek, 2, 9, 11

Gregory of Nanzianzum, 9-10

Gregory of Nyssa, 9

Gregory the Great, 9

Guardian Angel(s), 7, 15, 30, 32-33, 35, 45-46

Heavenly, 3, 7, 9, 20, 40, 43, 54, 57

Hierarchy, 9-10, 12, 14-15, 20, 28, 47, 59

Hinduism, 28

Holy, 3, 7-8, 11-13, 15-16, 20, 30-32, 40, 42-44, 46-48, 54-57, 63

Idol(s), 35-62

Idolatry, 39-40, 45-46

Invocation(s), 18, 33-35, 61, 65

Islam, 28

Jerome, 7-9, 59

Jesus, 3, 8, 10, 18-19, 40, 47-48, 55, 57

Jewish, 3, 8

Judaism, 28

Jungian, 28

Justinian (Emperor), 9

Karma, 33

Koran, 27

Lactantius, 7, 9

Luther, Martin, 13-16, 22, 46-48

Lutheran(s), 13, 46

Magic, 18, 46

Magicians, 18

Martyr, Justin, 7-9

Materialists, 1

Medieval, 11, 13

Messenger(s), 3, 7, 20, 29, 32, 44

Middle Ages, 11-13, 17, 21

Minister(s), 3, 7, 14-15, 19, 44-47, 55

Modern, 2, 18-19, 26-27

Modernism, 26-27

Moon, 40

New Age, 2, 27-28, 30, 32-33, 35-36, 46, 53-55

New Testament, 3, 7

Occult, 18, 20, 27

Old Testament, 2-3

Omnipotent, 42

Omnipresent, 14, 41-42

Omniscient, 42

Origen, 7, 9

Ouija, 1

Postmodern, 26-27, 36, 54-55

Postmodernism, 1, 26-27

Postmodernist, 26-27, 55-56

Powers, 3, 5, 12, 18, 21, 30, 41, 54, 59

Pray, 35, 40, 44-46, 56

Prayer(s), 9, 16, 18, 22, 33, 35, 42, 56

Praying, 16, 35, 42

Principalities, 21, 41, 59

Protestants, 13

Rationalism, 17, 19, 26

Reformation, 13, 17

Reformer(s), 13, 17

Relativism, 1, 26

Religious, 1-2, 8, 18, 27-28, 31, 40

Roman Catholic(s), 13

Rulers, 5, 16

Sacraments, 45, 48

Saints(s), 8-9, 20, 45, 47

Satan, 3, 13, 16-17, 25, 30-32, 42-43, 47

Schleiermacher, Friedrich, 18-19

Scholasticism, 11

Scholastics, 11, 13

Science(s), 18, 26

Scientific, 26

Scriptural, 3, 7-10, 16, 36, 39, 44, 47-48

Scripture, 7, 10-11, 13-14, 17, 19-20, 27, 39-41, 45-48, 54-55

Secular, 1, 16

Secularism, 1

Servant(s), 5, 7-8, 16, 19, 45, 48, 55-56

Sin(s), 3, 9, 11, 13-14, 16, 18, 40, 43, 48, 54, 57

Sinful, 16, 40

Sinned, 9, 13, 43

Sorcery, 35

Spells, 30, 33, 35

Spirit(s), 7-9, 14-15, 17-19, 26-28, 30-31, 33, 35-36, 40-41, 43, 54

Spiritism, 28, 39

Spiritual, 2-3, 7-8, 11-13, 16-20, 26-28, 30, 32-33, 36, 41, 43, 49, 55-56, 63

Spirituality, 12, 27, 32, 39, 53-56

Star(s), 2, 40, 65

Sun(s), 40, 63

Supernatural, 1, 26-27, 48

Swedenborg, Emmanuel, 17, 27

Syncretism, 27

Syncretistic, 27

Tatian, 9

Theological, 9, 12, 16

Theology, 2, 11, 15, 17, 19, 53, 55

Thrones, 5, 12, 21, 59

Universe, 30-31, 40, 42, 54, 56

Western, 1, 2, 25-27, 36, 54

Worldview, 1

Worship, 7-8, 10, 19-20, 35, 40-41, 44-47, 56, 62

Worshiped, 7-8, 16, 40, 44-45

Worshiping, 8, 39, 44

ACKNOWLEDGMENTS

I would like to express my sincerest thanks and appreciation, gratitude and love to my wife Jolene, and our children Julia, Liam, and Rowen, for their incredible support, encouragement, and especially patience. Without your love and understanding this would not have been possible. You stuck by me through all of the long days and even longer nights. God has richly blessed me through you. Each of you has been God's messenger of love and hope to me. May we continue to grow together in love and faithfulness toward one another and our Lord and Saviour Jesus Christ. To Him be all glory, thanks, praise, and honour.

All the angels were standing around the throne and around the elders and the four living creatures. They fell down on their faces before the throne and worshiped God, saying:
"Amen!
Praise and glory
and wisdom and thanks and honour
and power and strength
be to our God for ever and ever,
Amen!"
- Revelation 7:11-12

Sola Dei Gloria

About the Author:
Jacob Quast initially from Park Ridge Illinois, was raised in Stony Plain, Alberta. He later moved to Edmonton, Alberta where he researched angels thoroughly while completing a Master's of Divinity in 2003 at Concordia Lutheran Seminary. It was at this time Quast completed a master's thesis on the topic of Angels. Quast is married, with three children.

TODAY'S REFORMATION PRESS

www.todaysreformationpress.com
RR1 Site2 Box124 De Winton, AB T0L - 0X0

[ ] Please put me on Today's Reformation Press's email / mailing list
[ ] I would like to discuss authoring a book

Name: _____

Address: _____

City: _____ Province/State: _____

Postal Code/Zip: _____ Country: _____

Email: _____

Phone: _____

Comments: _____

_____

_____

www.ingramcontent.com/pod-product-compliance
Lightning Source LLC
Chambersburg PA
CBHW071312060426
42444CB00034B/2039